Murder By The Book

A Thriller

Duncan Greer

and

Robert King

Samuel French – London
New York – Sydney – Toronto – Hollywood

CHARACTERS

Selwyn Piper, a novelist
Christine Scott, his secretary
Imogen Piper, his wife
Peter Fletcher, his neighbour
John Douglas, his publisher

The action takes place in the drawing-room of Selwyn Piper's flat

ACT I   Early evening on a bright autumn day

ACT II Scene 1 The same. A few moments later
        Scene 2 The same. A few minutes later

Time—the present

A licence issued by Samuel French Ltd to perform this play does not include permission to use the Incidental music specified in this copy. Where the place of performance is already licensed by the Performing R Shr Society, a return of the music used must be made to them. If the place of performance is not so licensed then application should be made to the Performing Right Society, 29 Berners Street, London W1.

A separate and additional Licence from Phonographic Performances Ltd, Ganton House, Ganton Street, London W1 is needed whenever commercial recordings are used.

To The Masqueraders Theatre Club

ACT I

The drawing-room of Selwyn Piper's flat, situated near the top of an exclusive residential block of flats in North-West London. Early evening on a bright autumn day

The room has a small open balcony overlooking the surrounding area. There are three doors in the room: one the main access door, one leading to the bedroom and one to the kitchen and study. The flat is tastefully furnished and decorated. Essential furniture consists of a large sofa with a small occasional table in front of it, a drinks cabinet, a table on which stands a typewriter, and a record-player

As the CURTAIN *rises, Christine is typing. She is Selwyn's secretary, an attractive, likeable, efficient girl in her early twenties who displays unobtrusive charm. Although apparently devoted to Selwyn, their relationship never goes beyond that of employer and employee. She takes the paper from the machine and starts to tidy up*

Selwyn enters from the main door. He is a successful literary critic and thriller writer in his forties. He is well groomed, erudite and self-assured, with a ready but somewhat sardonic wit

Selwyn How's it going?
Christine Two chapters to go. I can break off for that review if you like.
Selwyn Which one?

Christine picks up a book

Christine The one by that new writer. *Death in Dunstable.*
Selwyn Must I?
Christine Unless you want to work over the week-end.
Selwyn Certainly not. Ready? (*He dictates*) Mr Preston's thriller completely held my attention—until the middle of chapter one.
Christine I see. It's going to be one of *those* reviews.
Selwyn A chapter which contained two split infinitives and, in addition to the inevitable homicide, many other examples of grammarcide. Full stop.
Christine Not an exclamation mark?
Selwyn Certainly not. An exclamation mark is a device for rescuing an ill-designed sentence. Where had I got to?
Christine Grammarcide.
Selwyn But let us forget—with some eagerness—Mr Preston's style and consider his substance. To begin with, there are no fewer than fourteen suspects, but, by a succession of further murders, the number dwindles rapidly to six. As these include the Home Secretary, the Dean of St

Paul's and the Headmistress of Roedean, I half expected to find that the crimes had been perpetrated by all three of these dignitaries in collusion.
Christine And had they?
Selwyn I haven't the faintest idea. I gave up half-way through. Where was I?
Christine In collusion, and getting ready for the *coup-de-grâce*.
Selwyn I regret to note that *Death in Dunstable* is published by my own publishers, Belton, Gleeson and Douglas. In fact I deeply regret that it is published at all. I regard the author as a threat to civilization second only to the Chinese Takeaway.
Christine You said that about the last book you reviewed.
Selwyn Did I? Then say: "the author is to the murder mystery what Nero was to Italian fire insurance".
Christine That's better.
Selwyn Thank you.
Christine You haven't used that one for more than a year. (*She picks up the book*) Good-bye, Mr Preston. It seems your first novel was also your last.
Selwyn You know I sometimes think I enjoy being a critic even more than I enjoy being an author.

Selwyn takes the book

Christine I'm not sure the two mix.
Selwyn I disagree. What could be better than to spend my afternoons killing off my victims and my evenings killing off my competitors? (*He drops the book in the waste-paper basket*)
Christine It does have its practical side.
Selwyn Too true. People read my vituperative essays and then buy my books to see if I can do any better.
Christine Which you usually can.
Selwyn Usually? Did I hear you say "usually"?
Christine No. I said "invariably".
Selwyn I should hope so. If ever they let me review my own work I shall say, "Selwyn Piper has raised literature to the level of the detective story".
Christine A neat twist.
Selwyn Neat twists are my forte.
Christine As a writer, not a critic.
Selwyn Granted. Neat thrusts are my critical forte. A talent I developed during my tempestuous marriage. In fact it was at my wife's suggestion that I became a reviewer.
Christine Really?
Selwyn Yes. It was one of the two things she did that I liked.
Christine You very seldom mention her.
Selwyn Imogen is definitely unmentionable.
Christine I can't believe that.
Selwyn But it's true. She was quarrelsome, selfish and drank far too much whisky.

Christine And she left you.
Selwyn That was the other thing she did that I liked.
Christine I know you hate predictable questions but why did you marry her?
Selwyn The best of us have lapses. She was mine. To be fair, I suppose she had her uses. She was a good business woman, at a time when I needed one. She had a private income, at a time when I desperately needed one. She bullied the publishers and made me work like a galley slave. She was an actress, you know.
Christine I didn't. Would I have seen her?
Selwyn She first trod the boards as Imogen Clark, but changed her name to Piper when I became a celebrity.
Christine Was she good?
Selwyn She gave the finest performance of Lady Macbeth I have ever seen. Unfortunately she was playing Juliet at the time.
Christine That explains why I'd never heard of her.
Selwyn She was well known in the business. She used to entertain lavishly —actors, angels, writers, producers, critics, agents . . .
Christine Parties?
Selwyn No, one at a time. While I was away.
Christine And you didn't mind?
Selwyn It diverted her attention at a time when I had a career to establish.
Christine I don't believe a word of that. If she was so promiscuous and you were so permissive, you must have been an ideal husband. So why did she leave you?
Selwyn We were always quarrelling.
Christine Even happily married people do that.
Selwyn Not like we did. We reached a point after which anything less than assassination would have been an anticlimax.
Christine Which, as a master of dramatic build-up, you had to avoid.
Selwyn Precisely.
Christine Then why didn't you leave her?
Selwyn I had nobody to go to. I rather gathered Imogen had.
Christine Another man?
Selwyn She was hardly the kind to fly off to a maiden aunt.
Christine You never knew whom?
Selwyn No.
Christine And you made no attempt to find out?
Selwyn To what purpose?
Christine I'd have thought it would be a challenge to your detective skills. Besides, you might want a divorce.
Selwyn But I don't. I've no intention of going through a costly and tedious procedure just to be free to repeat my error.
Christine That would be right out of character.
Selwyn Besides, I love frustrating Imogen. She phoned me the other day with an ultimatum. Divorce me—or else.
Christine Or else what?

Selwyn I don't know. She's probably working on it. She'll have got my reply this morning. It should give her apoplexy.

Christine Tut, tut! Vindictive.

Selwyn But enjoyable.

Christine That accounts for the sadistic streak which has crept into your new novel.

Selwyn What do you think of it?

Christine It's very ingenious.

Selwyn I'm always ingenious. But is it good?

Christine Yes, but—I liked the synopsis better.

A pause

Selwyn And how did you get hold of the synopsis?

Christine I found it somewhere—in your desk, I think.

Selwyn You know I don't like you to read my synopses. It blunts your judgement of the final product. Which I value.

Christine Then don't worry. It's a very good thriller. It's bound to be another best seller.

Selwyn Yes, that was my opinion—despite its one tiny flaw.

Christine A flaw? In a novel of yours?

Selwyn The hero should have called in the police the moment he discovered the body. (*His manner is unusually serious*)

Christine That would have ruined the whole plot.

Selwyn I know. But take my advice, Christine. If ever you're involved in similar circumstances, dial nine-nine-nine at once, won't you? It's not only sensible, it's free.

Christine I'll try to remember.

Selwyn I'm sure you will. I've never known you forget anything yet. In fact I'm dreading the day when that young man of yours decides to subject you to one of those revolting orgies of confetti and Mendelssohn.

Christine I can't quite see a choir in a Registry Office.

Selwyn Oh! Well, if it's that serious, you must present him to me.

Christine I will, some day.

Selwyn I'm very grateful for that advice you got from him on insurance practice—most useful for my next novel. I must meet him and give him a drink.

Christine I'll pass on your invitation.

Selwyn Of course, when you get married you needn't leave me. You could even move into the flat next door.

Christine Too late. It was let last month. Goodness! Look at the time. Ten to six and I've still the post to catch and your magazines to pick up.

Selwyn I'd forgotten. Friday routine. The last rites of the dying week.

Christine Don't forget your appointment at quarter-past.

Selwyn My dear Christine, I never forget an appointment with . . .

Christine John Douglas.

Selwyn With my publisher. Where is it? At his club?

Christine No, here.

Selwyn That's a pity.

Christine Why?

Selwyn We'll be up till midnight, talking shop for the first half-hour and golf for the rest.

Christine Then invent a dinner party later on.

Selwyn Brilliant! I'll do that.

Christine goes off through the main door, taking a pile of letters

Selwyn looks at his watch. He goes to the bedroom door, opens it, takes the key from the inside, locks the door and pockets the key. He goes to the kitchen door, locks it and pockets the key. He looks round the room as if checking. He puts his hand inside his jacket, gives a smile of reassurance, goes to the drinks cabinet and pours himself a drink. There is a ring at the main door. He opens it

Imogen enters, Selwyn's wife. A few years younger than her husband, she is an attractive ex-actress displaying theatrical charm and composure which often fail to conceal her strangely mixed feelings for her husband. At verbal fencing she is almost a match for him, but not quite. She is dressed in a suede jacket, jeans, and flat-heeled, soft-soled shoes. She wears dark glasses, which she takes off. She has a pile of blonde hair and is heavily made up

Imogen!

Imogen Dear Selwyn! Is that the best you can do? (*She mimics him*) "Imogen!" No choice epigrams. No vitriolic invective?

Selwyn As far as I'm concerned the name "Imogen" is a splendid piece of invective. But what are you doing here? You promised my doorstep you'd never darken it again.

Imogen That's a little better. I was beginning to think senility had finally caught up with you.

Selwyn On the contrary, I'm thriving. Sorry I can't say the same for you. You look positively autumnal.

Imogen Perhaps because the smile I gave you was intended to be wintry.

Selwyn My apologies. I took it to be an alcoholic leer. And why that extraordinary get-up? I didn't know it was Guy Fawkes Night.

He pours a drink while she surveys the room

Say "when", if the word doesn't stick in your throat.

Imogen When. A half-filled glass enhances the bouquet.

Selwyn You're thinking of wine, but the confusion is no doubt due to the volume you consume.

Imogen Neat.

Selwyn My joke or your whisky?

Imogen But a little disappointing. Too austere for a love nest.

Selwyn Don't pretend it's unfamiliar. I'm sure you've been scrutinizing it through a telescope ever since I moved in.

Imogen Wrong. I even had difficulty finding it. If it wasn't for that little card in the frame outside I'd probably still be groping about in the corridor.

Selwyn You're slipping.

Imogen Not really. I've been paying a little man to keep you under observation.

Selwyn What a shameful waste of money. I hope he told you the birds don't play in this particular nest.

Imogen Not openly. But he's waiting for the mating season.

Selwyn (*in mock horror*) You can't imagine that I'd make passes at my secretary!

Imogen Not even when the secretary's quite passable?

Selwyn You've seen her?

Imogen Just now. I watched her leave. From my car.

Selwyn You knew she'd be leaving at six?

Imogen Every Friday. She drives off like an automaton to catch the post and get your magazines.

Selwyn She'll be back shortly.

Imogen I know. In ten minutes' time. I shall leave a few moments before.

Selwyn You should stay. I'll introduce you to her.

Imogen No, Selwyn. You won't be in a position to.

Selwyn What do you mean?

Imogen Unless I can persuade you to change your mind.

Selwyn About a divorce?

Imogen Yes.

Selwyn Nothing doing. You received my letter.

Imogen I'm still seething.

Selwyn I'm so glad. And your means of persuasion? Not that I can imagine anything that . . .

Imogen We'll see, shall we? (*She produces a revolver*)

Selwyn Imogen! That isn't worthy of you. More to the point, it isn't worthy of me. Do you really expect me to give you your freedom at the point of a gun?

Imogen No, Selwyn. I expect you to refuse.

Selwyn Good.

Imogen Whereupon I shall take the utmost pleasure in shooting you.

Selwyn I don't believe you.

Imogen That I'd shoot you? Or that it would be a pleasure? But don't worry—I'll give you an even chance of survival. I shall shoot you through your heart.

Selwyn You little . . .!

Imogen Sorry it's such a prosaic end for a connoisseur of esoteric deaths. I know your predilection for tarantulas, blowpipes and iron maidens, but this isn't one of your murders. It's mine.

Selwyn All to be free of me.

Imogen There's the money as well.

Selwyn You're no longer my beneficiary.

Imogen Apart from my conjugal entitlement. And there's our joint insurance policy. I get one hundred thousand pounds when you die.

Selwyn Provided I've kept up the payments.

Imogen You have. I've checked. Now sit down.

Selwyn I refuse.
Imogen I'm not going to tell you again.
Selwyn How can I sit when you're standing?
Imogen I mean it, Selwyn!
Selwyn Don't be unsporting.
Imogen I always was. I prefer a sitting target. Sit!
Selwyn Oh, very well.
Imogen Good boy. Now—that door leads to the kitchen, doesn't it?
Selwyn Correct.

She almost tries the handle. He tenses

Imogen And from there to the fire escape?
Selwyn That's right.

She moves away. He relaxes

Imogen You appreciate my interest?
Selwyn Elementary. Your line of retreat.
Imogen It leads into a dark alley.
Selwyn Where you will undoubtedly look your best.
Imogen At the end of the alley is my car. I'm unlikely to be seen.
Selwyn Or heard. I suppose that's why you're wearing those sneakers.
Imogen You noticed?
Selwyn I'm a professional. But go on.
Imogen I'm a good shot as you know.
Selwyn Still go to the range?
Imogen Occasionally. I stick your photograph on the target.
Selwyn Charming!
Imogen That's probably why I haven't missed it for months.
Selwyn So you can promise me a quick death.
Imogen Yes. That's the only flaw in my plan. I still have the cottage so a few minutes after your death I'll be safely home in Hampstead.
Selwyn Where you'll immediately change into black.
Imogen What a lovely thought. Good suggestion, darling.

He moves towards her

   Don't move!
Selwyn (*freezing*) How will you dispose of the gun?
Imogen I shall leave it here by the body.
Selwyn Untraceable?
Imogen Absolutely. I acquired it ages ago. With you in mind.
Selwyn And your glass? Had you forgotten that?
Imogen I'm wearing gloves.
Selwyn You are also wearing lipstick.
Imogen Thank you. (*Puzzled, she starts to wipe the glass*)
Selwyn Stop it, you little fool. Haven't I taught you anything? Don't wipe it. Put it in your pocket and take it with you.
Imogen You're being incredibly helpful. You must have intimations of immortality.

Selwyn Only about my books. But I've made such a good living out of murder it would be churlish to cavil at finding myself the victim of one. Only not the victim of an amateur, please.

Imogen Very well. Any more professional tips?

Selwyn When you go down the fire escape, watch out for the people in the flat below. They're noise conscious and you don't appear to have brought your broomstick.

Imogen They go away every Friday afternoon and don't come back till Monday. My little man used that route to keep you under observation. You see, I've tried to be worthy of you.

Selwyn But even if you get away unseen you'll still be the principal suspect.

Imogen No, I won't. She'll be here with your body. In five minutes' time.

Selwyn Christine!

Imogen You seem concerned. Now you're beginning to realize I'm serious.

Selwyn You haven't the courage.

Imogen (*glancing out over the balcony*) Let's see, shall we? If I don't pull the trigger when I see her return, you'll be right. If I do, you'll have only a moment to contemplate your error.

Selwyn She has a key.

Imogen But she always rings first. She only lets herself in if you don't answer. By that time I'll be well on my way.

Selwyn What about the flat next door? They'll hear the shot.

Imogen I hope so. It would suit my book to have your randy little typist discovered alone with your body and my gun.

Selwyn And her motive?

Imogen Take your pick. A woman scorned. An expected legacy?

Selwyn A mere couple of thousand?

Imogen Perhaps she expected more. Wasn't she any good?

Selwyn Your little man can't have told you we were having an affair.

Imogen No, but John did.

Selwyn John? Not John Douglas?

Imogen Who else. And as he's due here in ten minutes' time he'll be able to keep an eye on things. By that time the police should be here.

Selwyn So it's John Douglas. You surprise me. He's far too ineffectual. What's in it for him? You?

Imogen And half the insurance.

Selwyn I wonder which he puts first. How long has he been . . .?

Imogen Long enough.

Selwyn He must have stamina as well as tolerance.

Imogen Or luck as well as judgement. There's her car now.

Selwyn So I've one minute to live.

Imogen I hope you won't be bored, darling.

Selwyn Supposing I yell "Imogen!" at the top of my voice?

Imogen Try it!

He opens his mouth. She aims the gun

And I'll shoot you now. What's up, Selwyn? Cat got your tongue?

Selwyn No. And as for the spineless, crapulous parasite, Douglas, you can tell him this. Every penny he makes comes from my work. He hasn't another writer on his books with enough talent to keep him in cigarettes, because he has the same instinct for picking ghastly authors as he has for picking ghastly women. He . . .

She shoots him twice. He collapses behind the sofa. Imogen puts the gun beside the body. She feels Selwyn's pulse and puts a lady's silk scarf in his hand. She blows him a kiss and goes to the kitchen door. She finds it locked and, in a panic, crosses to the bedroom door, finding that locked too. The bell rings. She picks up the gun. She changes her mind, puts the gun down again and opens the main door

Christine stands there with the key in her hand

Imogen (*in a Scottish accent*) I heard shots from the flat next door. Your telephone's out of order. I'd better go and ring for the doctor.

Imogen goes

Christine But . . . (*She sees the body and approaches it in horror*) Mr Piper, Mr Piper . . . (*She goes back to the main door*) It's no use ringing for a doctor . . . (*She sees the gun on the floor and picks it up*)

Peter Fletcher enters, dressed in trousers and a dressing-gown which reveals his apparently bare neck and chest. He is a young man in his late twenties, living in the flat next to Selwyn. At first he displays a light-hearted, frivolous manner and appears unable to take even the most solemn occasion seriously. During his most eccentric moments, however, he reveals flashes of acute intelligence which becomes more apparent as his character develops

Christine drops the gun

Peter I say, excuse me, but I'm from the flat next door. I think I've over-slept. It's not really six o'clock, is it?

Christine half collapses in his arms

I only asked for the time. (*He sits her down on the sofa*) Phone. (*He makes for the telephone*) No, brandy. (*He sees the body*) Good Lord!
Christine She's ringing for a doctor, but it's no use. He's dead.
Peter (*feeling Selwyn's pulse*) Yes, I'm afraid he is. Is this your gun? That explains the sounds I heard. I didn't like to say that's why I came in, in case they were just champagne corks popping, only there were two of them and it's unusual to open two bottles at once, isn't it? What happened?
Christine I think he was shot.
Peter I think you're probably right.
Christine I'd just come back. I'd . . .
Peter What you need is a good stiff drink. May I?

Christine nods

I'm having a triple Scotch. What's yours?

Christine Anything.

Peter I think brandy's your best bet. It's the ideal drink when you've just found a body. At least I think it is. I've never really found one before. Er—does he live here?

Christine Yes.

Peter And you?

Christine No, I'm his secretary, Christine Scott. I'd been out posting his letters. When I got back . . . You must ring the police. No, you can't— the telephone's out of order.

Peter You sit down and drink this. There, knock it back. I thought you said there was someone doing a spot of phoning for you.

Christine Yes. The woman who was here when I came back. Your wife, I suppose.

Peter No, it couldn't have been my wife.

Christine Why not?

Peter I haven't got one.

Christine But she said she lived next door.

Peter I'm the only one next door and I live alone. Mind you, when I took the flat they did say it was full of amenities. Of course, I follow your reasoning. This woman says she lives next door and I turn up half undressed, so you assume I'm married to her, but it doesn't necessarily follow. I mean I could be half undressed and not married to her. Anyway I'm wearing a shirt. (*He opens his dressing gown*) See? I always tuck the collar in when I'm shaving or it gets covered in soap. Haven't you noticed that? No, I suppose not. (*He picks up the scarf from Selwyn's hand*) Any idea whose this is?

Christine Yes. It's mine.

Peter Oh dear.

Christine I lost it last week.

Peter Well he seems to have found it.

Christine I'm . . .

Peter It was in his hand.

Christine I . . . I . . .

Peter I think you'd better have a refill. What did she look like?

Christine Who?

Peter The lady phoning the doctor. The one I'm living with without knowing it.

Christine Oh. She was wearing a suede jacket. And jeans. She had dark glasses.

Peter Ah!

Christine And she had a Scottish accent.

Peter That clinches it. She was definitely lying. I'd never share a flat with a Scottish accent. (*Offering her a drink*) Here.

Christine No, thank you.

Peter Go on, take it.

She takes the drink

Good. Now. Was she short or tall?

Christine I think she was rather short.

Peter Stand up a minute.

Christine Shorter than I am.

Peter Then she was exactly five feet two.

Christine How do you know?

Peter You're about five feet four. If she were only an inch shorter you wouldn't have noticed. Had she been three or four inches shorter you wouldn't have been in any doubt.

Christine That's very clever of you.

Peter Yes, I suppose it is really. Have you cheered up a bit?

Christine A little.

Peter Splendid. Cheering up damsels in distress is my speciality. Now I hate to return to a rather morbid subject, but who is—was . . .?

Christine Selwyn Piper.

Peter You don't mean Selwyn Piper, the crime writer?

Christine Yes.

Peter But this is absolutely marvellous! I've read everything he wrote. I've always wanted to meet him. (*His face falls*) Only now that I have it looks as if I never will. Yes, I've been a Piper fan for years. I always put the book down just before the last chapter then I pop into bed and lie awake until I've worked it out. Then I get up and finish it to see if I was right. Fantastic, isn't it? For a whole month there's only been that wall between Selwyn Piper and me and I never knew it. (*His manner suddenly becomes serious*) You're in a bit of a mess, aren't you?

Christine Yes, I suppose I am.

Peter You didn't kill him, did you?

Christine No, I didn't.

Peter Thank goodness for that. Not that I thought you did. You're far too obvious. You were alone with a body, looking disgustingly guilty, your scarf in the dead man's hand . . . We've got to find another suspect —it's our only hope.

Christine But . . .

Peter Don't argue. Leave everything to me. Now the first possibility is that I did it.

Christine You?

Peter Well I've just turned up from nowhere.

Christine Next door.

Peter You mustn't be so trusting. I've no motive, no connection with the corpse. In a book I'd turn out to be the murderer every time. I'm not, mind you, but I'm such a good bet that I'm almost surprised that I'm not. But I've let you out, so it's only fair you do the same for me. And who does that leave?

Christine The woman.

Peter Suede jacket and glasses. You rang the bell . . .

Christine And she opened the door. She said she'd heard shots. Then she went to phone for a doctor.

Peter When did you discover the phone was out of order?

Christine I didn't. She told me it was.

Peter Ah! A clue. (*He picks up the receiver*) Just as I thought. A perfectly beautiful dialling tone. She's a very naughty lady. Was she wearing gloves?

Christine Yes, I think she was. White gloves.

Peter You handled that gun, didn't you?

Christine I picked it up.

Peter Are you *sure* you typed his novels?

Christine I wasn't thinking clearly. It was a reflex action.

Peter My God! We can't let you go to court—you won't stand a chance. You must have some idea who she was.

Christine No . . . Yes, I might have.

Peter Well?

Christine Imogen!

Peter Who?

Christine Imogen Piper. His wife. They're separated, but she telephoned him the other day, demanding a divorce—or else. And he refused.

Peter He told you this?

Christine Yes.

Peter There we are—everything fits! She wanted a divorce. There's her gun and she came here disguised. Motive, opportunity, means. It's a perfect case. (*His face falls*) It must have been somebody else. Had he made a will?

Christine Yes.

Peter Does his wife get anything?

Christine I don't know.

Peter Did he leave you something?

Christine Me?

Peter Why not? I would.

Christine Well yes. He did, actually.

Peter How much?

Christine All I know is he told me he'd made a new will and mentioned me. It's looking worse, isn't it?

Peter Never mind. With any luck he may only have left you the typewriter. I say, I hope you find another job.

Christine Thank you.

Peter You could come and work for me, if you're stuck, but the trouble is I don't do anything. I'm one of the idle rich—well not rich actually. I suppose I'm one of the idle medium. Where does she live?

Christine Who? Oh! Imogen. She has a cottage in Hampstead.

Peter Hampstead. What's her phone number?

Christine I don't know. Why?

Peter If she's the one she'll be home by now, won't she?

Christine Would she go home?

Peter I always go home after I've killed someone, don't you? Where does he keep his phone numbers?

Christine There's a little book on his desk. It's in the study. Through there.

Peter Oh yes, I know. This flat's the same as mine only back to front.

Bedroom over there. Rest of the flat through here. That's funny. Does
he always keep his door locked? (*He pulls at the door in vain*)
Christine Is it locked?
Peter If it's not I'm incredibly weak. The key's not here. I wonder . . .
That's the bedroom you say?
Christine Yes.
Peter (*trying the door*) I thought as much.
Christine Locked too?
Peter You get an instinct about these things. Well, this explains why
Dark Glasses and Suede Jacket didn't use the fire-escape to get away.
She had to face you and bluff it out. Cool, very cool.
Christine I really think we ought to ring for the police.
Peter What on earth for?
Christine Aren't you supposed to when there's been a murder?
Peter Yes, but there's no law that says you've got to do it right away.
Christine But they'll want to know why we waited.
Peter Simple. Dark Glasses said she was going to phone them, didn't she?
Christine But Mr . . .
Peter Fletcher, Peter Fletcher. How do you do?
Christine We must ring the police. It's . . .
Peter Miss Scott, you have two things in common with the Mona Lisa.
You're beautiful. And you've been framed.

Pause

Christine I don't know how I can make you believe me, but I'm . . .
Peter Innocent. I know. That's an essential condition for being framed.
Almost certainly by Imogen Piper, whom we are now going to ring.
Now, we can't get to his phone numbers in the study. There's only one
thing for it—the telephone directory. Sometimes I scintillate.
Christine Look—we can't just ring her.
Peter Stop being so negative. Of course we can. (*Looking through the
directory*) Piggot—Pike—Pilkington . . .
Christine What are you going to say to her?
Peter I'm not saying anything. You are.
Christine Me?
Peter Here we are. Piper—Imogen. Four-two-six two-one-one-e-oh. When
you say Selwyn wants to see her she won't know what to think. She'll
be desperate to know what's going on. You've got to panic her. Now
keep calm and get a grip on yourself. Do you do deep breathing exer-
cises? You know—childbirth without pain—that sort of thing?
Christine No.
Peter Well now's the time to start. Speak with authority. A spot of subtle
menace. It's ringing.
Christine Can't you . . . ?
Peter Shush! It's answered. (*He gives her the receiver*)
Christine (*on the phone*) Hullo? Is that Mrs Piper? . . . Mrs Selwyn Piper?
. . . This is Mr Piper's secretary. He would like you to come round here
as soon as possible . . . To his flat. . . .

Peter More menace.

Christine (*on the phone*) It's a matter of life and death. He says he has to see you here—now. . . . No, you can't speak to him, Mrs Piper. He's lying down at the moment. . . . I'm sorry; I can't tell you any more.

Peter It's to her advantage.

Christine But it's to your advantage.

Peter Threaten.

Christine Mrs Piper, I honestly do advise you to come. I think you might regret it if you didn't. . . . Thank you. (*She puts down the receiver*) She'll be here in a few minutes.

Peter Now it's my turn to have another drink. Did you recognize the voice?

Christine Not Scottish.

Peter Of course not. Right, what we do now is wait.

Christine And when she arrives?

Peter Don't worry, I know exactly what we'll do. We'll improvise. If she's not the one, we'll just break it to her gently . . .

Christine And if she is?

Peter Then we'll call the police. The one thing they're awfully good at is arresting people. Do you know, I'm thoroughly enjoying this? Oh, I say, I'm sorry. That must have seemed absolutely heartless. Will you forgive me?

The doorbell rings

Now who the devil's that?

Christine What time is it?

Peter Six-twenty.

Christine Then it's John Douglas.

Peter Who's he?

Christine Mr Piper's publisher. I'd completely forgotten. He had an appointment at quarter-past. Shall we let him in?

Peter I don't know. He deserves to be kept waiting. He's five minutes late.

Christine He won't go away. Not with an appointment.

The doorbell rings again

Peter No. Hold on. (*He moves the sofa to hide the body from anyone viewing it from the main door*)

Christine Aren't you going to tell him there's been a murder?

Peter That depends. Don't you think it's a coincidence that he should have an appointment now? Anyway, open the door. Say I'm your friend.

Christine (*looking at his dress*) I think he'll assume that.

Christine opens the door

John Douglas, Selwyn's publisher, enters. He is a bluff, middle-aged, immaculately turned-out bachelor with an easy charm which disintegrates into bewilderment under stress. He is intellectually inferior to both Selwyn and Imogen and often fails to appreciate the import of the deadly games they play on each other. As a result he becomes a pawn in their hands

John Good evening, Christine. How have you been keeping? Is Selwyn still working you hard? I hope so, because . . . (*He sees Peter*) Oh!

Christine This is a very good friend of mine—Peter . . .

Peter Fletcher.

Christine John Douglas.

John How do you do?

Peter How are you? Excuse me, I'll just pop off and slip a jacket on.

John Yes . . . (*To Christine*) Where's Selwyn?

Peter Who?

John Selwyn.

Peter Ah! Good question. Excuse me.

Peter goes off through the main door

Christine Mr Piper had to go out. Something turned up quite suddenly.

John Will he be back soon?

Christine I'm not sure. Mr Fletcher will know.

John Will he?

Christine I'm sure he will.

John I take it he's gone *home* for his jacket?

Christine Yes, he has. He lives next door.

John I see. Have you known him long?

Christine A while.

John Yes, I suppose you must have.

Christine Let me get you a drink.

John Thank you.

Christine I'm sure he won't be long.

John Who? Your very good friend, or Selwyn?

Christine Both. It is pink gin, isn't it? With no ice?

John Yes. I say, I hope Selwyn remembered my appointment. I was beginning to think I'd got the right time but the wrong author. (*He laughs nervously*)

Christine Actually it's right author, wrong time.

John I beg your pardon? Oh, I see what you mean. I'm five minutes late.

Christine Er—how's the golf?

John The golf? Oh, not too good, I'm afraid. I've been so damned busy lately. The other day someone asked me what my handicap was and I said "work". What was it that turned up?

Christine I beg your pardon?

John You said something had turned up. Quite suddenly. I was wondering what it was.

Christine I'm sure you were. I know I am. You see, he didn't tell me.

John He just left?

Christine Yes.

Peter enters. He has taken off his dressing gown and carries his tie and his jacket

Peter There. Wasn't long, was I? Excuse me while I put on my tie. I always dress for dinner.

John Of course. Are you also a very good friend of Selwyn's, Mr . . .?

Peter Fletcher. No, I'm more of an admirer. Of his books, you know.

John As his publisher, I can safely say I do know.

Peter Yes. Belton, Gleeson and Douglas. Would you mind?

He gives John his jacket. John takes it, looking stupefied

John Have you any idea where he's gone?

A pause while Peter considers the metaphysical implications

Peter No. I don't know him well enough.

John It really is most important that I see him. There's his new book to discuss and the film rights of . . . (*He takes his drink from Christine*) Thank you. Look, there's nothing wrong is there?

Peter Why? Should there be?

John No, of course not. But you seem to be . . . Nothing's happened, has it?

Peter Excuse me. Is my tie straight?

John It's about the only thing that is.

Peter Thanks. Mr Douglas, are you sure you wouldn't prefer a brandy?

John No. Pink gin's my drink at this time.

Peter Let me get you a brandy. (*He takes John's drink*)

John What the . . .! I don't want a brandy.

Peter I think you're going to need one. (*He pours a brandy*)

John Why the hell should I need a brandy?

Peter Because although you've published hundreds of murder mysteries, it might come as rather a shock to find yourself in the middle of one. And for cases of shock I prescribe brandy rather than pink gin. (*He gives John the brandy*)

John But . . .

Peter Thank you. (*He takes his jacket from John and slips it on*)

John Look, I don't know what the devil you're up to . . .

Peter I know, and it must be infuriating, but you see . . . (*He leads John into a position where he can see the body*) There.

John Good God! (*He gulps down the brandy*)

Peter Same again?

John What—what happened?

Peter He was shot.

John Shot?

Peter With a gun.

John When?

Peter Less than twenty minutes ago.

John My God! Is he dead?

Peter We'd hardly leave him down there if he wasn't, would we? (*He picks up the gun*) Have you seen this before?

John No, I haven't. And you shouldn't be handling it. You'll destroy the fingerprints.

Peter There aren't any. The murderer wore gloves.

John How on earth do you know that?

Christine I saw her when I came back from posting . . .

John You saw her? A woman?

Christine Yes.

John Imogen!

Peter Why Imogen?

John I don't know. She was his wife. She's an actress. Very temperamental. They didn't get on. I gather she'd been pushing him to divorce her.

Peter You're very well informed.

John Look, who are you anyway?

Peter I live next door.

John I know, but aren't you carrying the good neighbour policy a little too far?

Peter I'm intrigued by the criminal mind.

John You're not with the police?

Peter Certainly not. I'm a gifted amateur detective and I'm one of your best customers.

John Just the same, I'd prefer a policeman at the moment, even if he happens to be illiterate. I take it you've phoned the police?

Peter No. We're going to eventually, but we haven't got round to it yet.

John goes to the telephone

Not just yet if you don't mind.

John stops and stares at Peter

We're expecting a visitor. The murderer. At least I think it's the murderer. In fact we all seem to have the same idea, don't we?

John Imogen?

Peter Yes.

John But she can't . . .

Peter She can't what, Mr Douglas?

John How do you know she's coming here?

Christine I just phoned her.

John You did what?

Peter She engaged her in telephonic communication. Science is a wonderful thing, isn't it?

John I don't—I meant . . .

Peter Yes, Mr Douglas, what do you mean?

The doorbell rings

Ah! Excuse me. (*He opens the door*) Mrs Piper?

Imogen (*off*) Yes.

Peter Won't you come in?

Imogen enters. She is taller, in high-heeled shoes. She is now a brunette, having removed her wig. She is smartly dressed and discreetly made up. She is scarcely recognizable as the woman Christine saw

Imogen Thank you.

Peter Miss Scott, may I introduce you to Mrs Piper? Or have you already met?

Pause

Imogen I don't believe so, have we? But I have a dreadful memory for faces. (*To Peter*) I don't recall having met you either, and you have such an interesting face.

Peter I'm Peter Fletcher. I live on the other side of that drinks cabinet.

Imogen How nice for you. (*Moving to John*) John! What a lovely surprise to see you again.

John How are you, Imogen? It's been a long time.

Imogen Far too long. But you haven't changed a bit. Still the same charming John. And you're wearing the tie I gave you a few Christmases ago.

John Am I? So I am. It really is a very nice tie. And you're looking younger than ever.

Imogen Dear John, you always did say the sweetest things.

John No, it's true.

Imogen I was going to the opera actually.

John Really? How nice. Which one?

Imogen Actually it's . . .

Peter Forgive my interrupting this fascinating reunion, but we do have an urgent matter to discuss.

Imogen Have we?

Peter That's why you came.

Imogen I came in response to a very odd telephone call from Miss . . .

Peter Scott.

Imogen She was very cryptic, and a trifle importunate.

Peter Mrs Piper, please sit down.

Imogen If you wish. (*She hesitates, seeing that the sofa has been removed, then sits*)

Peter I think this room's been arranged rather well, don't you?

Imogen I've hardly had time to notice it.

Peter You haven't been here before then?

Imogen No, never. Now will someone please tell me what all this is about? Where is Selwyn?

Peter Ah! I was wondering when you were going to ask that.

John Now look here, Fletcher . . .!

Peter She's been told Selwyn wanted to see her urgently. Then she arrives here to find not Selwyn but three other people, yet it takes her a good two minutes to get round to asking where he is.

Imogen And what do you infer from that?

Peter That you already know where he is.

Imogen Nonsense. I haven't seen him in ages.

Peter Yet you spoke with him a few days ago.

Imogen How do you know?

Peter People tell me lots of things. I'm an extremely good listener.

John Well, all you've done since I've been here is talk.

Peter And now it's Mrs Piper's turn to talk.

Imogen And I refuse to talk to anyone but Selwyn. Where is he?

Peter Behind the sofa.

John Fletcher! (*He goes to Imogen*) For God's sake, Imogen! He's dead.

Imogen Dead? Selwyn? No!

Peter Someone shot him. See for yourself.

John Don't be so damned callous, Fletcher.

Peter My dear Douglas, Mrs Piper's not exactly a broken-hearted widow. Let her take a look and see that divorce is no longer necessary.

John That's a disgusting thing to say.

Imogen Yes. It's true I wanted to be free, but not that.

Peter Well, someone wanted that.

Imogen John, get me a drink, would you please?

John Of course.

Peter And I believe that someone was Mrs Piper.

Imogen Me?

Christine But she's not at all like the woman I saw.

Imogen You saw a woman?

Christine Yes. Mr Piper was lying there dead and she opened the door for me.

Imogen But she was nothing like me?

Christine No. She was fair, and shorter than you.

Peter And Scottish.

Christine And I think she was younger.

Imogen I'm sure you mean less sophisticated. Has someone phoned the police?

Peter Our mystery woman said she'd do all the telephoning and we've no reason to doubt her, have we? (*He sits next to Imogen*) You don't mind, do you? Tell me, John . . . You don't mind if I call you John, do you?

John Yes, I do.

Peter Tell me, John—did you notice Mrs Piper's reaction when she spotted the sofa?

John I beg your pardon?

Peter No, of course you didn't. Silly question. Mrs Piper, when I asked you to sit down, do you know what you did?

Imogen I sat down.

Peter Before that.

Imogen I contemplated sitting down.

Peter No, you hesitated. Because you suddenly realized that the sofa had been moved.

Imogen How could I possibly realize that when I've never been here before?

Peter Which brings me to my next question. How did you find your way here?

Imogen Since I drive half way round Europe every year locating a street two miles from my home is hardly a miracle of navigation.

Peter I mean to this flat. There are two flats on this floor—this one and

mine, and neither of them is numbered. How did you know which one
to go to?

Imogen By a card on the door.

Peter A card saying "Selwyn Piper"?

Imogen Exactly.

Peter Which you read just now?

Imogen Yes.

Peter goes to the main door, opens it and takes out the card

Peter Then perhaps you'd like to read it again.

Imogen looks at it

John Well, what does it say?

Imogen "Peter Fletcher".

Peter It was quite a simple trick really. I swopped Selwyn's card for mine
when I went out for my jacket. There was just a chance she wouldn't
glance at it if she'd been here earlier.

Christine Then it was you.

Imogen I'd like that drink please.

Peter Is that a confession?

Christine It is whisky, isn't it, Mrs Piper?

Imogen Who told you that?

Christine Selwyn—Mr Piper told me.

Imogen What an odd piece of information to impart to one's typist. Then
I'm sure you don't need me to tell you to make it a large one. Neat if
you don't mind.

Peter Not at all. It's normal for the condemned prisoner to be granted
any reasonable request.

Imogen Oh come, Mr Fletcher. Surely I'm not condemned yet? The case
for the defence hasn't been heard.

Peter You have a case?

Imogen Of course. (*She takes her drink from Christine*) But I'm not obliged
to present it to you.

Peter Then I suggest that you shot your husband and tried to throw
suspicion on Miss Scott.

Imogen And how did I do that?

Peter By pinpoint timing. You arrived while she was out. You shot
Selwyn just before she returned and you reckoned on getting home and
changing from your obvious disguise before the police popped round to
break the news.

Imogen Mr Fletcher, it would be very difficult to drive from here to Hampstead, change from my "obvious disguise" and drive back all within
twenty minutes.

Peter I don't know. You're an actress. You . . . Just a moment. How do
you know it took twenty minutes?

Imogen I don't know.

Peter That's funny. I could have sworn she said twenty minutes, couldn't
you, John?

Imogen I was judging from the time Miss Scott phoned me.

Peter But how could you have known how long after the murder that was?

Imogen It was only a guess, Mr Fletcher.

Peter I wonder what inspired it?

John Fletcher, do you mind if I say something?

Peter Yes.

John Christine, I'm only looking at this from the legal angle, so I hope you won't take it personally, but the fact is that we've only got your word to go on that there was a woman here at all.

Christine And you don't accept my word?

John Of course I do, my dear, but I don't think that really matters, because I don't come into it.

Peter Don't you, John?

John No.

Peter I can't help wondering about that.

John Wonder away, old man.

Peter Your behaviour hasn't been entirely free from oddity.

John That's rich, coming from you.

Peter But I'm an odd chap generally. Your oddness stands out like a penguin in a row of nuns. To have timed her actions to the minute as Mrs Piper did . . .

Imogen Could have done.

Peter She'd have needed to know a good deal about Selwyn's routine. The question is: how did she know?

John Certainly not from me. I knew very little of Selwyn's routine. I was only here, oh . . .

Christine Once a fortnight.

John Well, perhaps. But anyway I haven't seen Imogen for years. Yes, it must be. Years.

Imogen You really have neglected me quite shamefully.

Peter And isn't it a coincidence that you're here, now, by appointment?

Christine One which you asked for.

John Now really . . .

Peter Don't take it personally, old man. She's only looking at it from the legal angle.

John I protest at this ridiculous attempt to implicate me.

Peter But if you had planned everything with Imogen it would be jolly useful to be on the spot just after the police. You could give them a prod in whatever direction you wanted.

John This has gone far enough.

Peter If you found that line in a novel you'd refuse to publish it. Miss Scott, when Selwyn told you about Mrs Piper, did he say whether she had a special boy-friend?

Christine Well—he thought she wanted a divorce to marry someone else.

Peter Are you a bachelor, Douglas?

John What the hell has that to do with you?

Peter I've got an aunt who's getting desperate. Yes, John, the police will

do their damnedest to establish a connection between you and Imogen.
Do you think they'll succeed?

John No, they won't.

Peter Ah! You've been too discreet.

John Nothing of the sort.

Peter Then you haven't been discreet.

John I will not answer any more of your impertinent questions. I've only
put up with them so far for Imogen's sake, because I am sure she is as
innocent as I am.

Peter Yes. That's the conclusion I'm coming to. You say you haven't seen
her for years?

John Yes.

Peter Then would it be fair to say that you hardly ever think of the lady?

John More or less.

Peter Yet when I told you there was a woman here the first thing you
said, and I quote, was "Imogen"!

Pause

Imogen Did you, John?

John It's understandable, isn't it?

Imogen I suppose you were assuming that when there isn't a butler, the
principal suspect is invariably the wife.

Peter Of course he might have asked Miss Scott to describe the woman.
That might have told him whether it was you or not.

Imogen But he didn't?

Peter No, he didn't.

Imogen Why not, John?

John I don't know. I was upset, I suppose.

Peter You were upset all right. You were shaking like a jelly the moment
you came into this room. But I don't actually say you killed him,
because you wouldn't use a gun. You're more of a knife man.

John Right! That does it. I wouldn't say any more if I were you. The
next communication you receive from me will be through my solicitor.

Peter Could I recommend my uncle? He's awfully good.

Imogen Neither of us is going to need a solicitor. There isn't a shred of
evidence against either of us.

Peter Except those two little slips you made.

Imogen All you can infer from your little "card trick" is that I've been
here before.

Peter So you admit it?

Imogen Yes. I came last week to try and see Selwyn.

Peter Ah!

Imogen But there was nobody in so I went away again.

Peter is incredulous and almost childishly frustrated

Peter That isn't fair! You've just thought that up.

Imogen No, Mr Fletcher. I've just decided to tell you. As a concession.
But I don't have to tell you anything else. I am going to call the police.

Peter You don't want the place crawling with police. Not before dinner anyway. It's a mistake to be interrogated on an empty stomach, as you've just discovered, no doubt. I'm sure your itinerary didn't allow for a stop at a neighbouring Wimpy. I'll tell you what. Can you cook?

Imogen Superbly.

Peter Then would you mind rustling up some omelettes or something? I'm sure there must be some eggs in the kitchen.

Imogen I can't. The ...

Peter The door is locked. Yes, Mrs Piper, we found that out, but it's reassuring to learn that you've discovered it as well. Slip number three. Perhaps we'd better give you and John a chance to get your stories sorted out.

John We don't ...

Peter Yes, John? You were about to say?

John Nothing.

Peter Yes, you've been saying a lot of that all evening. Come on, Christine. Let's go and have a bite to eat while the conspirators conspire.

John You can't leave us alone with Selwyn.

Peter He won't look. And if we're wanted we'll be in that little Indian restaurant round the corner.

Christine But ...

Peter No buts. Be a good girl and get your coat. A tactical withdrawal is just what's called for. And, John, take my advice. Plead guilty and settle for manslaughter. Imogen, you phone the police. We'll be back shortly ready to face the whole of Scotland Yard, and—*(assuming an Indian accent)*—very, very full of poppadums.

Peter and Christine go out

Imogen You bloody fool!

John Me? You've been giving yourself away every other sentence.

Imogen Stop talking like a publisher. God! Why were those doors locked?

John Does it matter?

Imogen If you'd been stuck here with a dead body instead of waiting on the touch line, you'd have thought it mattered.

John That isn't fair. I've been rather more than a spectator.

Imogen Yes, but on whose side? When you were told that damned girl had seen a woman, why did you say "Imogen"? And don't tell me it's because I'm the only woman you ever think about.

John It was quite involuntary. I realized something had gone wrong, that you must have been discovered. Naturally I was shocked. Blast Fletcher! God knows what we're going to do now. *(He goes to the balcony)*

Imogen And what about that scarf?

John Scarf?

Imogen Christine's scarf. The one you stole. The one which I put in Selwyn's dead hand.

John It isn't there now, is it?

Imogen I can see that, you idiot! Locked doors. Vanishing scarves. Mystery men from next door. It's like one of his books. It's as if ...

(*She feels Selwyn's pulse*)

John What are you doing?

Imogen (*checking his pulse*) That's a relief. I was beginning to think the bastard was still alive.

John Do you mind, Imogen? That remark was in singularly bad taste.

Imogen You hypocrite. We've just murdered him. I suppose you think that was in singularly good taste.

John All the same, he was your husband. (*Looking out over the balcony*) There they go, crossing the street.

Imogen And now he isn't.

John Isn't what?

Imogen Alive. I'm free at last.

John Damn! They've gone out of sight.

Imogen Well, thank you for the wild enthusiasm.

John Oh, for God's sake, Imogen! This is a fine time to ask me to register pleasure. I thought you were proud of your sense of timing.

Imogen You know I'm beginning to wonder about you.

John Me?

Imogen Yes, you.

John You're upset. You're not thinking clearly.

Imogen I'm thinking very clearly. We planned everything so perfectly. Why did it all go wrong?

John I don't know. I wish to heaven I did.

Imogen You still want to marry me, don't you, John?

John Look here, Imogen . . .

Imogen Answer me!

John What do you want me to do? Go down on my knees? Shall I put on a Mantovani record?

Imogen I was beginning to wonder whether your share of Selwyn's life insurance wasn't more attractive to you than his beneficiary.

John Don't be ridiculous—you know I care for you. I was sick with worry while I knew you were here with Selwyn. I was imagining what I'd do if something went wrong—if he somehow got the gun from you and . . .

Imogen Shot me? That would have been interesting. He would have got the hundred thousand.

John Would he?

Imogen It's a joint policy.

John Oh, yes. I'd forgotten. Look, let's have another drink.

Imogen Why not?

John Did you have your whisky when you got home?

Imogen Why?

John I just wondered. I left one for you as usual, poured out on the table.

Imogen There wasn't time. I'd just got back when the phone rang. So I did a lightning change and drove here like mad.

John I think that was a mistake.

Imogen I don't run away from trouble. You'd have been on a jet to South America by now. That's the modern way of deserting the sinking ship isn't it?

John Am I such a bad catch?

Imogen I'm beginning to re-evaluate you, my dear. And I detect a distinct lack of backbone.

John Selwyn had that, and you left him.

Imogen And little Christine moved in. I don't know how I kept my hands off her.

John Why should you care that she was having it off with Selwyn? You didn't want him.

Imogen That doesn't mean I wanted anyone else to have him.

John What a strange attitude.

Imogen It would be to you. You treat sex like an H.P. agreement. So much down and once a month thereafter.

John You're very ungrateful. It was I who told you they were carrying on.

Imogen I wish you hadn't. Then none of this would have happened. (*She goes to the telephone*)

John But it has. So what do we do now?

Imogen Send for the police and bluff it out? (*She picks up the receiver*)

John What else can we do?

Imogen I don't know. I can't make up my mind.

Selwyn (*rising from behind the sofa*) Then let me make it up for you.

CURTAIN

ACT II

SCENE 1

The same. A few moments later

Selwyn Delightful. Most satisfying. Nothing more than a strangulated gasp. I'm so pleased. I've always avoided putting screaming women in my books.

Imogen Selwyn . . . You should be dead.

Selwyn Forgive me, darling, but is that opinion moral or metaphysical?

Imogen I shot you.

Selwyn Ah! Then it's metaphysical. Yes, you did, and it was beastly of you. Yet here I am, alive and unharmed. Or am I? Would you like to touch me to make sure it isn't ectoplasm? Not even going to wish me many happy returns? Ah, well, that's death. Would you like to know how I did it? Was it a bullet-proof vest? Did you just miss? Or perhaps mind triumphed over matter. But just to prove I'm not a ghost, I'm going to have a drink. I think champagne is appropriate, don't you? (*He takes a bucket containing an opened bottle of champagne with a patent removable stopper. Clearly, it has been prepared for the occasion and kept out of sight*) Convenient, don't you think? Or evidence that I was expecting this celebration? You'll know your aim was as good as ever if it starts to gush forth from my chest like a drinking fountain. You'll join me of course? After all one drinks at a funeral so why not at a resurrection?

Imogen Thanks. I'll stick to whisky.

Selwyn What a pity you're not as faithful to your men as you are to your booze.

Imogen So it was you who locked the doors.

Selwyn Mean of me, eh?

Imogen Then you know everything.

Selwyn I usually do.

Imogen But who—how?

Selwyn Another mystery. Was I hiding in your chest of drawers? Did I secrete a tape recorder under your bed? Now there's an erotic thought. But you'll pardon a novelist's habit of prolonging the suspense. Champers, for you, John?

John No thanks, Selwyn. It gives me heartburn.

Selwyn How romantic. But you really must on this occasion.

John Oh, very well. I thought you were never going to wake up. How do you feel?

Selwyn A bit stiff, but apart from that, hale and heartless.

Imogen I see. Well, that explains who.

John Imogen. I . . .

Imogen Now all I need to know is why and how.

Selwyn How?

Imogen How I could have missed you from that distance.

Selwyn Cheers, everyone.

Imogen You're not gushing forth champagne. My hand must have trembled with ecstasy.

Selwyn Yes, darling, it usually did. But not on this occasion enough to make you miss from a few feet. (*He picks up the gun and points it at Imogen*)

John Selwyn, please . . .

Selwyn It's all right. I'm just showing our good lady where she went wrong. Now you stand over there, darling, and play me.

Imogen Am I that good an actress?

Selwyn Apart from your Juliet. Now there are four rounds left, if I remember correctly. However, one will suffice.

Imogen What are you up to?

Selwyn Come now. Courage. Exit with a smile. You're playing Selwyn. And don't move, my sweet. I'd hate this moment spoiled.

Imogen So would I.

Selwyn As a markswoman first class would you say that this gun is pointed at your chest, preferably a trifle to the left of centre?

Imogen Give or take an inch.

Selwyn Good. I've a passion for accuracy.

John Selwyn, could I have a word with you?

Selwyn Later.

John But we haven't worked out . . .

Selwyn Later! (*To Imogen*) Good-bye, darling.

Imogen Selwyn, you can't!

Selwyn Why not? You did.

Imogen Selwyn!

Selwyn fires. Imogen gasps, clutches her breast and staggers. She collapses to her knees, then recovers

Oh! God!

Selwyn You see? Blanks. You'll be all right in a minute. I was. I'll get you some more of your highland medicine.

John That wasn't very funny, Selwyn.

Selwyn I thought it was rather droll.

Imogen You . . .! You . . .!

Selwyn You obviously need lubricating. You know this affair has already cost me more whisky than I normally get through in a month. Oh, don't look so reproachful. It wasn't half as bad as what you tried to do to me.

Imogen I loaded that gun myself last night.

Selwyn (*throwing down the gun*) And John unloaded it this morning. And reloaded it with blanks. Isn't he a little charmer?

Imogen So instead of falling down dead—
Selwyn I fell down alive. Sit down, John. You make the place look untidy.

John sits

Imogen I checked. I felt your pulse.
Selwyn So did everybody else. I felt like a National Health patient in a teaching hospital. Even the eccentric Mr Fletcher checked. But I was prepared for that. When I fell, which you'll agree, I did most convincingly, I landed so that one arm was tucked under my body, while the other—this one—was temptingly outstretched.
Imogen That's the one I felt.
Selwyn You should have known better than to trust me, even in death.
Imogen How do you get rid of a pulse?
Selwyn By cutting off the flow of blood to the artery in question. Let me show you. (*He unbuttons his jacket*)

She steps back

Don't worry. I'm not going to insist on my conjugal rights. Not in front of John, anyway. Here, strapped to my armpit by a piece of stout plaster, is a small rubber ball, directly over the brachial artery, the one that pulsates at the wrist, you know.
Imogen I didn't, but I'll take your word for it.
Selwyn Now, when I press the upper part of my arm against my side the rubber ball squeezes my artery against the humerus, the bone at the top of the arm—so—cutting off the supply of blood to the wrist. It works on the same principle as the Kariba dam. Result—no pulse. Care to feel?
Imogen I'll take your word for that too.
Selwyn I spent weeks perfecting the technique in my bath. I can turn it on and off like a tap—or a tourniquet. (*Holding out the ball*) Care for a souvenir?

Imogen shakes her head

Pity.
Imogen You do love your little games, don't you? Do you still play *Scrabble* and *Monopoly* until the early hours?
Selwyn I gave them up when you left me. After all, it was the stakes we played for that made them such fun. Another drink for you, John, my friend?

John shakes his head, pointing furtively to his own glass and indicating the door

John No. I . . .
Selwyn Isn't it nice to have friends?
Imogen How would you know?
Selwyn By observing the happiness they bring to others. You, for example, look radiant.

Imogen Stop it, Selwyn. You've told me how you did it. I want to know why.

Selwyn Certainly. John, if you're not going to join in the festivities go and take a walk round the block, there's a good chap. I really would like a word with your—with my . . .

John Oh yes—well—right. I'll see you later then.

Selwyn We'll look forward to that.

John Quite. Well, cheerio, Imogen.

John goes

Selwyn Isn't this ironic? The complete reversal of our situations. But I'm forgetting my manners. Let me refill your glass. (*He does so and hands her the drink*) There! Make yourself comfortable and relax. I must say now that you're decently turned out, you don't seem to have changed much. You're even wearing the same perfume.

Imogen So are you.

Selwyn Nonsense. It's my new after-shave.

Imogen In my honour?

Selwyn But of course.

Imogen Mine's not in yours.

Selwyn Don't tell me you're wearing it for John. What a waste. I don't believe John has the stamina to cope with you.

Imogen Why didn't he just walk out?

Selwyn I've no doubt his legs were willing but his spirit was weak.

Imogen So he came to you with the whole story.

Selwyn Tragedy.

Imogen Were you surprised?

Selwyn Agog, my dear. You'd misjudged your man, you know. I'm afraid the insurance money wasn't sufficient compensation for having to put up with you for the rest of his life. But taken by itself, fifty thousand is a nice little nest egg. So, to use a metaphor which I'm sure is dear to the poor fellow's heart, John was on the horns of a dilemma. He needed someone to lean on.

Imogen So he turned to you.

Selwyn Like a babe to its mother. I offered him a solution with three advantages. First, by not killing me he would retain the talents of his best-selling author. Secondly, my solution meant the end of his affair with you. And, thirdly, he'd still get his fifty thousand pounds.

Imogen (*puzzled*) Sounds brilliant, but expensive.

Selwyn Not at all. I made him the same offer as you did. Only in my version, you were cast in the role of the corpse.

Imogen (*shaken*) That's a role I've never played.

Selwyn Oh, but you have. Remember your Juliet?

They look at each other

(*Laughing*) You really are admirable. You're determined not to ask about my murdering you—but of course you're still drinking it in. Excuse me.

Selwyn unlocks the door to the kitchen and goes off

Imogen looks suspiciously at her whisky, and hurriedly puts the glass down on the coffee-table in front of the sofa

Imogen Selwyn, I lived with you, if you can call it living, for some years and I know that you're dying to tell me, just as I'm longing to hear. (*She takes a sinister-looking paper-knife from her handbag and hides it behind a cushion on the sofa*) All right, darling. Please tell me how you're going to murder me.

Selwyn enters from kitchen with a whisky bottle, wrapped in tissue

Selwyn Was going to.

Imogen Why the past tense? Has my presence rekindled the spark?

Selwyn Flame, my sweet, flame.

Imogen So that's how you're going to do it—incineration.

Selwyn Let's just say that my method was one which would make the police think that you had taken your own life.

Imogen But you won't tell me what it was?

Selwyn No—I may want to try again. (*He strokes her hair*)

Imogen Would our insurance company pay out on suicide?

Selwyn Certainly, on a policy as mature as ours. Christine checked with a boy-friend in insurance. I told her it was background material. Anyway, although the police would assume suicide, I was confident of an open verdict at the inquest.

Imogen So you have a rival?

Selwyn A rival?

Imogen For your typist's extra-curricular services. The boy-friend.

Selwyn Good Lord, no. I've not met him but she says he's charming.

Imogen You mean you haven't . . .

Selwyn Certainly not. I would never let sex come between Christine and me. Her shorthand's far too good.

Imogen But John said . . .

Selwyn I know he did. That was another mendacious embellishment—

Imogen —to lull me into a false sense of security—

Selwyn —by suggesting an alternative suspect—

Imogen —with a plausible motive.

Selwyn You know it's such fun to talk with someone who can truly appreciate my Machiavellian ways. You really are pure Borgia.

Imogen Thank you.

Selwyn Tell me—who does your hair nowadays?

Imogen A sweet little Spaniard in Curzon Street.

Selwyn Did he also provide the wig you wore earlier, or was that a souvenir from your summer season in Bridlington?

Imogen It was part of my disguise.

Selwyn Disguise? You looked about as inconspicuous as an Arab in a synagogue. Fletcher saw through it, at once.

Imogen Apparently.

Selwyn An intriguing chap, Fletcher. I must admit he gave me quite a turn when he arrived. I didn't dare come to life until he'd departed.

Imogen How are you going to explain your reincarnation? You know, it's funny. I always thought you'd come back as some sort of weasel.

Selwyn Dear Imogen. I'm just beginning to realize how much I miss the subtlety of your intellectual bludgeon.

Imogen Forgive me, my love. You know how I use shallow jokes to hide deep emotions.

Selwyn Ah yes—I must say that is a most becoming dress. (*He is beginning to find her physically attractive*)

Imogen Darling, thank you. Does that mean you want me back?

Selwyn For two or three days in the year—and perhaps four or five nights. I don't believe you've ever been more challenging. Or felt more inviting. Soft, very soft.

Imogen Or, as you used to put it, yielding.

Selwyn Not always yielding. I used rather to enjoy the fights.

Imogen We were so beautifully matched.

Selwyn There isn't much fight in old John, is there?

Imogen No, it's rather like hitting a pillow.

He moves to the record-player

What are you doing?

Selwyn Nothing sinister. (*He puts on a record of "Bye-bye Blues"*)

Imogen Soft music. That's going a bit far, isn't it? But you always were one to gild the lily.

Selwyn "Paint", my sweet. "Gild" is one of your frequent misquotations. (*He goes to the balcony and looks out*)

Imogen I never was very good at Shakespeare.

Selwyn So your Romeo told me. Which reminds me. Have you seen the exquisite view from my balcony?

She tenses, realizing the implications of the question

Imogen Briefly.

Selwyn Magnificent, isn't it?

Imogen Not especially.

Selwyn You used to be quite romantic about balconies.

Imogen Really?

Selwyn And it is such a perfect evening. Come and see.

Imogen Remind me, darling. How many floors up are we?

Selwyn One from the top.

Imogen And how many from the bottom?

Selwyn Oh dear, such cynicism!

Imogen I'll stay here if it's all the same to you, darling.

Selwyn What's on your mind, darling?

Imogen The same as what's on yours, darling, but from the opposite angle.

Selwyn Imogen really! Did you think I was trying to lure you here to— that I'd actually contemplate push . . . I'm ashamed of you.

Imogen (*rising*) Then I'll give you the benefit of the doubt.

Selwyn Ah!

Imogen (*moving further away from the balcony*) From here.

Selwyn Honestly, I . . . What's amusing you?

Imogen (*laughing*) This situation. It's so ludicrous. Is it from one of your books?

Selwyn I'll have you know that even in my most fanciful books there is nothing which could be described as ludicrous.

Imogen Except your picture on the back cover.

Selwyn (*moving close to her*) Remember how you used to admire them in the old days?

Imogen When we were living on your talent and my money.

Selwyn Even genius takes time to establish.

Imogen I established you.

He puts his arms round her

Selwyn Yes, I'll grant you that.

Imogen Do you remember the time we were still in love?

Selwyn Yes—I seem to recall it was a Tuesday. Seriously darling, I remember every little episode. A woman in love goes into ecstasies. A man in love goes into details.

Imogen Who said that?

Selwyn I think I did. You were ecstatic, passionate, inventive, destructive and insatiable. Who was it said a woman spoils her first lover and ruins the rest?

Imogen I don't know, darling, but that is the loveliest compliment I've ever been paid. And you were always high up in the ranks of the rest. Thank you. (*She kisses him*) Why don't you divorce me? Then we could have such a beautiful affair.

Selwyn I have my public image to think of, and you have such a deplorable taste in co-respondents. Why don't you divorce me? It's easy enough nowadays.

Imogen But with my Messalinic record as a wife and your spotless reputation as a husband I doubt if I'd have got anything but a fat legal bill. So you see, dear, I had to kill you. It was nothing personal.

Selwyn I know the feeling.

They dance to the music with the easy relaxation of true lovers

Imogen Darling?

Selwyn Yes, darling?

Imogen Please tell me how you were going to kill me.

Selwyn No, darling. It would spoil this precious moment.

Imogen But I'm dying to know.

Selwyn Very well put.

Imogen You love a game of cat and mouse, don't you?

Selwyn Cat and dog, my dear. I have to prevent the cat from striking again. (*He caresses her neck*) Remembering your instinct for hit-and-run, I'd never have an easy moment crossing the street.

Imogen You might not be much safer on the pavement.

Selwyn Yes, I remember your driving. The trouble is I can't decide whether you deserve death or the fate which they say is even worse.

They kiss. The telephone rings

Imogen Aren't you going to answer it?

Selwyn How can I? I'm still dead. (*He goes to the record-player and takes the record off*)

Imogen Are you?

Selwyn Very. It's part of my plan.

Imogen Oh, you still have a plan then?

Selwyn Answer it for me, will you? Don't say anything. Just repeat the caller's name.

Imogen Certainly, darling. (*She answers the telephone*)

Hullo?... Oh, hullo, John Douglas. How lovely to hear from you John Douglas... Certainly, John Douglas. (*To Selwyn*) It's John Douglas.

Selwyn Give it to me.

Imogen But he may want to speak to me. (*On the phone*) Poppet, do you want to speak to me?... Very well then, I'll give you Selwyn. Do hurry back. There's so much I want to say to you.

Selwyn (*on the phone*) Yes?... Are you? Good. Did you remember the...? Good. And the...?... Well done... Right. 'Bye. (*He replaces the receiver*)

Imogen That was most illuminating.

Selwyn It was meant to be most obscure.

Imogen Well, what did you...?

Selwyn No more questions. Let's enjoy ourselves until Fletcher gets back.

Imogen What are you going to tell him about your renaissance?

Selwyn That it put an end to the Dark Ages. You know, I don't know what I'd have done without John. Even now he's completing a vital errand. (*He straightens a cushion, sees the knife, and secretes it in his pocket*) That's why he phoned.

Imogen Where is he?

Selwyn At your cottage.

Imogen Doing what?

Selwyn It's safe to tell you now. He's disposing of the suicide trap we set for you.

Imogen (*sitting on the sofa*) That's funny. I didn't notice any trip-wires or trap-doors.

Selwyn No. We had something more insidious in mind. Poison.

Imogen Oh? In my tea?

Selwyn We couldn't wait for you to die of old age.

She drains her glass

In your whisky.

She reacts

Forgive me. Not the whisky here. The whisky at your place.

Imogen I must remember to replace my stock.

Selwyn Oh, it's all perfectly safe except for the one glass which Christine's telephone call saved you from drinking. You're empty. Let's drink to our mutual failure. I think I'll join you in a Scotch. (*He crosses to the drinks cabinet*) What's the matter, dear? You look shattered.

Imogen When John cultivated that custom of leaving a drink poured out for me I thought it was an affectionate joke.

Selwyn No, it was a macabre one.

Imogen And a part of your sneaky plot.

Selwyn A most important part. (*In view of the audience but unseen by Imogen, he puts something into one of the drinks*) If we'd poisoned an entire bottle it wouldn't have been consistent with suicidal practice. (*He hands her one drink, places the other on the coffee-table in front of the sofa, then moves to the record-player*)

Imogen So after polishing you off—or so I thought—I'd return home and knock back the poisoned whisky . . . Suppose I hadn't noticed it?

Selwyn Objection definitely overruled. (*He puts on a non-vocal record of "They Can't Take That Away From Me"*)

Imogen Presumably it was one of those odourless poisons your books utilize so monotonously. (*She smells her own drink*)

Selwyn (*with his back to her*) Naturally.

She quickly exchanges her glass for his

Imogen What about the supporting evidence? The bottle the poison was in?

Selwyn All catered for. John planted one at your cottage.

Imogen I wonder why you went to all that trouble? You could have doctored my drink at any time.

Selwyn Imogen, please. You really have been living amongst the Philistines. A Selwyn Piper creation must have shape and style. Your death had to be connected with a suicidal impetus.

She toys with her glass. He watches her intently

Imogen And what better impetus than a fit of remorse for murdering you. (*She raises her glass to her lips*)

Selwyn Right. When you realized the blow you'd dealt to English culture you decided to deal an equally heavy blow to Scottish commerce.

She puts down her glass untasted

Imogen But you weren't dead!

Selwyn (*trying hard to suppress his impatience*) As long as you thought I was.

Imogen I see. Or do I?

Selwyn (*raising his glass*) In vino veritas.

Imogen (*raising hers*) Cheers! (*She is about to drink, but changes her mind and puts the glass down*) Why the locked doors?

Selwyn (*edgily*) Christine had to find you here with my body. You see, if Fletcher hadn't turned up she'd have phoned the police at once and told them about you.

Imogen But she didn't know it was me.

Selwyn That didn't matter. She saw a woman. She'd describe her to the police. Suede jacket. Dark glasses. Jeans. The police would be round at your place in a flash.

Imogen And find . . .

Selwyn The suede jacket, jeans . . . Unless you'd stripped off in the car. Which is extremely inadvisable on Hampstead Heath.

Imogen So Christine's evidence would corroborate yours?

Selwyn Quite. And the knowledge that you'd been rumbled . . .

Imogen Would provide a second motive for my suicide.

Selwyn You're improving already. Cheers, darling!

She is about to drink, but again changes her mind

Imogen Oh, Selwyn. I hate to admit it, but you really are clever.

Selwyn (*now almost frantic at her reluctance to drink*) Thank you, I think so too. I conceived the whole thing as though it were my latest thriller. I even typed out a synopsis. Thank you for providing some of the plot. (*Fiercely*) Your health!

A slight pause. Her glass is poised near her lips

Imogen But it's all gone wrong, hasn't it?

Selwyn Plots can be changed. Only certain characters are immutable.

Imogen You know, we've both been far too oblique. The next time I try to do you in I shall simply push you off a cliff. Shall we revisit Eastbourne this summer?

Selwyn If I do, I'll send you a suggestive postcard. Cheers!

They both drink. There is a pause. They both start to laugh

Imogen What are you laughing at, darling?

Selwyn I have a small quantity of those pills put by for emergencies.

Imogen What pills?

Selwyn The poison. I've just put one in your drink.

Imogen laughs

What are you laughing at, darling?

Imogen I switched the glasses.

Selwyn begins to laugh

What are you laughing at, darling?

Selwyn I knew you would.

She drops her glass. She searches for the knife

Have you lost something, darling? (*He shows her the knife*)

Imogen You're lying. You must be.

Selwyn (*taking the bottle from his pocket*) Here's the empty bottle. (*He looks at his watch*) You should be going any moment now.

CURTAIN

Scene 2

The same. A few minutes later

Selwyn, presumably having carried the body into the bedroom, enters and blows Imogen a kiss. The record of "They Can't Take That Away From Me" is still playing. He goes to the occasional table and picks up her handbag. He takes the knife and the poison bottle from his pocket, wipes them and puts them into the bag. He wipes the bag and takes it and Imogen's glass, holding them in handkerchiefs into the bedroom. He re-enters and pours himself some champagne. He collects a dish of nuts and sits on the sofa eating them. He raises his glass to Imogen. He picks up a magazine and, noticing the cover, "Life", smiles. The doorbell rings. He looks at his watch, takes off the record, surveys the room and answers the door

John enters, goes to the drinks cabinet, pours himself a drink and gulps it down

Selwyn Well?

John Everything's fine.

Selwyn The poisoned whisky?

John Down the sink. (*Proudly*) And I washed up the glass.

Selwyn You clever little devil, you! Have some champagne.

John No thanks. Heartburn, you know.

Selwyn Of course. I forgot.

John Any sign of Fletcher?

Selwyn No, but if he really went to that Indian restaurant he should have finished his curry by now.

John I don't like it.

Selwyn Neither do I; it's an acquired taste, I believe.

John Where's Imogen?

Selwyn She's through there, laid out on the bed.

John I'm not surprised. She's been through a hell of a lot in the past hour.

Selwyn Rather more than you imagine.

John What?

Selwyn She's dead.

John Dead?

Selwyn I killed her. Poisoned her whisky. (*He drinks appreciatively*)

John My God, Selwyn . . . !

Selwyn My dear fellow, you appear shocked. Isn't it what we always intended?

John You fool! You'll never get away with it.

Selwyn The question is not whether *I'll* get away with it, but whether *we* will.

John I had nothing to do with it.

Selwyn Then go to the police and say, "I took part in the first attempt to kill Imogen, which, I'm pleased to say, failed, but I took no part in the second attempt, which unfortunately succeeded". I can just visualize their constabulary cynicism.

John But I wasn't even here. I was at Imogen's.

Selwyn Prove it.

John How can I?

Selwyn Do as I tell you and everything will be all right. The plan is exactly the same. She committed suicide. The only thing that's changed is the venue.

John I refuse to have any part of this.

Selwyn Very well. I shall tell the police that you killed her. It'll be my word against yours and I'm much more convincing than you are.

John You bastard! You . . . !

Selwyn That'll do, John. You've no choice. We stick to the same story about my return to life.

John And where was I when Imogen died?

Selwyn Here.

John You mean I actually saw her do it?

Selwyn No. After Christine and Fletcher left, Imogen confessed to my murder. She seemed one degree under, so you suggested she went into the bedroom to lie down. Then I recovered from my faint and, after you'd recovered from the shock, you went into the bedroom to tell Imogen and found her dead.

A pause, while John concentrates miserably

John I'll never convince anyone; I've only just learned the first story.

Selwyn Don't worry, I'll be here, holding your hand.

John I don't like it.

Selwyn I was speaking metaphorically. But you don't have to like it. Just do it.

John But—but how did she take the poison?

Selwyn In her Scotch, just as before.

John And the blanks in the gun? Is that the same story?

Selwyn Just as we rehearsed it. (*Offering the dish of nuts*) Have a nut?

John Something's bound to go wrong.

Selwyn With any luck.

John What?

Selwyn I thrive on the unexpected. And there is an unexpected quality about my next-door neighbour.

John You're mad, Selwyn. Stark, staring, bloody mad.

Selwyn I dispute that. I just happen to believe that there's no fun in playing snakes and ladders without a healthy preponderance of snakes.

The doorbell rings

Answer that for me, will you?

John The locked doors! What about the locked doors?

Selwyn Don't fuss. All catered for.

The doorbell rings again

Go on. Answer it.

John admits Christine and Peter

Selwyn launches into a swift, voluble speech designed to overwhelm Peter and establish mastery

Peter Fletcher, I presume. Please forgive the solecism, but this really is like the moment when Stanley met Livingstone. John told me all about you. I can't thank you enough for your sterling efforts on my behalf. If ever I do get murdered I shall instruct my executor to send for you immediately. Your incisive reasoning, your implacable cross-examination, your intuitive intellectual leaps! Are you real? Are you sure I didn't invent you? I do apologize for the shock I've just given you. Have a nut.

Peter is utterly bemused, and answers mechanically

Peter No, I've just had a curry.
Selwyn Oh, what was it like?
Peter (*staring at Selwyn*) Hot.
Selwyn Yes, John here prefers it milder. Did you enjoy your meal, Christine?
Christine I don't understand, Mr Piper.
Selwyn What? Oh, why I'm—(*he indicates a standing position*)—instead of—(*he indicates a prone position*). Oh, the explanation's quite simple. Christine, come and sit down. You too, Mr Fletcher.
Peter No, thank you.
Selwyn Oh? Never mind. Where were we?
Peter Your quite simple explanation.
Selwyn Oh, yes. Imogen's gun was loaded with blanks.
Peter That was jolly thoughtful of her.
Selwyn No, it was jolly thoughtful of John. The dear fellow suspected she was going to use it on me.
John From something she said—
Selwyn —in her sleep.

John and Selwyn stare at each other, Selwyn beaming, John looking bleak

So he took a humane precaution for which I shall be eternally grateful.
Peter (*to John*) But how did you manage it? You haven't seen her for years.
John Well, yes, I know, but . . .
Selwyn Did you tell him that, John?
John Yes, I'm afraid I did.
Selwyn I suppose it's quite understandable. We're all a little shy of admitting adultery.
John Quite.
Selwyn You see, Christine; the other man—cuckolded by my own publisher, and I didn't know it. You can imagine the mixed feelings I now have for him. Now, Christine, you'd like some champagne, wouldn't you? Mr Fletcher? Splendid! Champers all round. Except for poor John—it gives him heartburn. Slosh it around, there's a good fellow.
Peter Tell me something, Mr Piper.

Selwyn Anything.

Peter Were you awake the whole time?

Selwyn No, of course not. You see, I didn't know about the blanks, so when I saw Imogen begin to squeeze the trigger there was only one thing to do. So I did it. I threw myself aside in a balletic leap.

Peter And?

Selwyn And I remember nothing after that. I must have struck my head on something.

Peter Any bruises?

Selwyn I don't bruise easily.

Peter How fortunate. (*Suddenly*) Did Imogen feel your pulse?

A slight pause. Selwyn smiles appreciatively at him

Selwyn How would I know? I was unconscious. But they're tricky things, pulses. And Imogen isn't a trained nurse.

Peter I felt it.

Selwyn Are you a trained nurse?

Peter Well, let's see if your wife can confirm your story? I take it she's gone home?

Selwyn Not exactly.

Peter Where is she?

Selwyn In the bedroom.

Peter moves towards the bedroom door

I wouldn't go through there if I were you.

Peter Why not?

Selwyn Something terrible has happened. Imogen is dead.

Christine Oh no!

Peter goes into the bedroom

John May I help myself to another brandy, Selwyn?

Selwyn Certainly, old boy, and I haven't got my champagne yet. Believe me, Christine, I can't say how sorry I am that you've been caught up in this wretched business.

Christine What happened to her?

Selwyn We're not absolutely sure but she evidently died before I came to.

Christine But you were here, weren't you, Mr Douglas?

John Yes, that's so . . .

Christine Well?

John In a way, yes.

Selwyn Better make yours a double, old man. You were telling us about Imogen.

John Was I?

Selwyn No, but I feel sure you were going to.

John Oh, yes . . . Well, she said she felt faint, so she went into the bedroom to have a rest.

Selwyn And, alas, it seems she was referring to "the final rest".

Christine How horrible.

Selwyn In spite of what she tried to do to me I couldn't be more upset. May I please have my champagne? As you know, I wasn't particularly fond of her, but even so, she was my wife. (*To John*) You must be feeling this more than any of us.

John Indeed—indeed I am.

Peter enters

Peter You're quite right. Mrs Piper is dead.

Selwyn Is there anything to show how?

Peter There's a whisky glass by her side, and a small empty bottle.

Selwyn You've examined the glass?

Peter Yes.

John Probably poison.

Selwyn That was the conclusion I came to, John.

Peter When did you find her?

Selwyn I didn't. John did. After he discovered I was alive.

Peter (*to John*) And the shock drove you straight to the bedroom?

John Well—not exactly . . .

Selwyn He went to break the news gently to Imogen. After all, if she'd suddenly been confronted with my spectre the poor lady might have had heart failure.

John Of course, we didn't know that she was already dead.

Selwyn True, very true.

John It's a terrible business.

Selwyn It is indeed.

Peter How did she get into the bedroom?

John She just walked in.

Peter But the door was locked.

John Was it?

Peter It was when I left less than an hour ago.

Christine That's true.

Peter Did she have a key?

John Well, as a matter of fact . . .

Selwyn She did.

Peter Her own key?

Selwyn No, mine. She took it from my pocket when she went to lie down.

Peter How do you know she did? You were unconscious.

Selwyn John told me. He saw her take it.

John That's right. That's exactly right.

Peter How odd!

Selwyn What is?

Peter Her knowing the key was in your pocket.

Selwyn Not really. You see, she'd seen me put it there . . . But let me explain.

Peter Surprisingly enough, I was going to.

Selwyn Quite. Before she shot me we'd been quarrelling. I'd begun to find her presence tiresome. I asked her to leave. She refused.

Peter You could have booted her out.

Selwyn My dear fellow, I am a gentleman. And stratagems are so much more satisfying.

Peter And what was yours?

Selwyn I said if she wouldn't leave, then I would; and I locked the kitchen door as I invariably do when I'm leaving the flat.

Christine But you don't lock the bedroom door.

Pause

Selwyn I've just started to.

Christine Why?

Selwyn To stop you rifling my desk, my dear.

Christine I never do that.

Selwyn Oh yes, you do. You told me so this evening. You read the synopses of my books, even though you know it infuriates me. So you see, there's no mystery about the locked doors.

Peter No, but there's still the very strange mystery of the gun.

Selwyn I don't follow you.

Peter (*to John*) Mr Douglas?

John (*startled*) Yes?

Peter You put the blanks in Mrs Piper's gun.

John Yes—yes, I did.

Peter Then why, when you first saw Mr Piper on the floor, did you believe he was dead?

John I did think he was dead.

Peter Why?

John drinks

John I beg your pardon?

Selwyn He asked why you thought I was dead. Tell him.

John Fletcher said so, for one thing.

Peter But you thought he'd been shot by Imogen and Imogen's gun contained blanks.

John Well, how was I to know he hadn't been killed some other way?

Peter You saw the gun there?

John Yes.

Peter The gun which you'd rendered harmless?

Selwyn Perhaps he thought I'd been clubbed to death with the butt.

John Yes, something like that. (*He laughs nervously*)

Peter Rubbish! You recognized that gun as Imogen's.

John No—yes—well, I . . . No!

Peter Why not?

John I don't know.

Peter But you only unloaded it this morning.

John Yes, I did. But I didn't know the shooting had anything to do with Imogen.

Peter But you mentioned her name.

John Involuntarily.

Peter A sure sign you connected her with the murder.

John I admit the thought did cross my mind.

Peter Then why didn't you check to see if he really was dead?

John I don't know—I . . .

Peter Because you know damn well he was alive.

John But . . . (*He rushes over and pours another drink*)

Selwyn Never mind, John. You know, that is a remarkable assumption, Mr Fletcher.

John Oh, he's full of assumptions—wild ones. Why, you heard him yourself, earlier on.

A pause, as his mistake sinks in

Selwyn I wish I had. But I was unconscious, was I not?

John Yes, you were. I'd forgotten.

Christine Well, Mrs Piper's part in the affair started as an assumption—now it's a fact.

Peter So I've no doubt my latest theories will prove equally true.

John What are these theories?

Peter That you became her accomplice and then you double-crossed her.

John I'm damned if I'm going to stay here and listen to this.

Selwyn Easy, John, easy. (*To Peter*) Peter—may I call you Peter?—I rather think you are basing too many conclusions on the premise that John here is capable of consecutive thought.

John Precisely.

A pause, while they stare at him and he realizes the inane quality of this remark

Selwyn You see? But don't let me put you off. As a novelist I'm finding this most riveting. I can't wait for your opening chapter.

Peter That begins with Douglas telling you of Imogen's plot to kill you.

Selwyn That sounds more like a prologue, but pray continue.

Peter Chapter two reveals your counter plot.

Selwyn Which was . . . ?

Peter To let your wife think she'd killed you and then poison her to make it look like suicide.

Selwyn Absolutely brilliant. Fictionally speaking, of course.

Peter Then you'll love this next bit. Douglas was in the habit of leaving drinks poured out for her. The one he left this evening was poisoned.

Selwyn And yet she managed to return here alive?

Peter Yes. Because she didn't drink it.

Christine My telephone call must have saved her.

Peter But it was left for her all the same.

Selwyn How can you be sure of all this?

Peter You don't really think we went to the restaurant, do you?

Selwyn Ah!

Christine We waited round the corner in my car until Mr Douglas came out and got into his. We followed him.

Peter To your wife's cottage. Where, from the side lawn, we could see right into the kitchen.

Christine (*to John*) You poured the whisky down the sink, washed the glass, left the house and drove away.

Peter We gave him five minutes and then came back here.

Christine To find his car parked outside.

Selwyn You have been a busy little bee, haven't you, John?

John What do you mean? It wasn't ...

Selwyn Shush.

Peter All of which adds up to attempted murder and casts considerable doubt on the story you've just told us about Imogen's suicide.

Selwyn Well, well, Peter, I congratulate you. You have a hyperactive imagination from which you have conjured up a most extraordinary thesis. Yet the only evidence you have is that John was seen to clean up a glass in Imogen's sink. Perhaps he's a compulsive dishwasher.

Peter You're wrong. There's this. (*He produces some typed pages*)

John What is it?

Peter A synopsis of the whole story from start to finish—just as I've described it—with the exception of your ingenious improvisations. Found by Christine six weeks ago, and quite by accident, in your desk. This is a photocopy.

John You—you've—you've done something very serious, young man.

Selwyn I should have locked that door months ago.

Peter Yes, you should.

Selwyn So you two have known each other for some time?

Christine Yes, we have.

Selwyn And he's not simply the man from next door.

Peter I'm the man from next door, but not simply. Christine told me when the flat became vacant and I moved in.

Selwyn To spy on me?

Peter Well, to be on the spot.

Selwyn But I still don't understand. Surely your misgivings were not aroused simply by reading the synopsis of one of my novels?

Christine It wasn't only that. A day or so earlier you'd wanted that information about insurance. You knew I had a friend in that line, so you asked me to find out about suicide clauses.

Selwyn So this is the boy-friend. The affianced. Congratulations, Christine. I'm sorry, you were saying?

Christine Peter did some checking and found that you and your wife held a joint policy with his company.

Peter "Ah!" I thought. A coincidence.

Selwyn Yes, I agree.

Christine So I kept my ears open. Particularly when you and Mr Douglas were together. It finally fell into place when I heard your phone call to him yesterday, telling him that today was the day.

John Oh dear.

Peter So there it is. We knew everything all along. I'm delighted our performances convinced you we didn't. Of course, to persuade you I was capable of some odd behaviour I had to play the part of an eccentric.

Selwyn Have you stopped?

Peter Just about. But you were equally good in your part as the corpse. Pity it had such a short run.

Selwyn Very good. But apart from an evening's free drinking, what was your purpose?

Peter It was all for Christine's sake. You see she has a certain loyalty to you.

Christine Yes, I have.

Peter Why, I don't know. She didn't want you to go to prison. But you had to be stopped. How? I needed more proof—I couldn't go to the police. Our evidence was too insubstantial.

Selwyn I'm sorry to appear dense, my dear fellow, but what evidence?

Peter The synopsis.

Selwyn scoffs

Admittedly a few pages of a murder plot might have been just an idea for a novel.

Selwyn Clever of you to have noticed that.

Peter I considered telling you I knew everything.

John But you didn't, did you?

Peter No. It would have stopped you for the time being. But I wanted the deterrent to be a more lasting one.

Selwyn Why should that have concerned you?

Peter It would have concerned my father. He's my Company's chairman.

Selwyn You should go far. So you let me go on with my dastardly plot until you had proof positive.

Peter Now I'm in a position to persuade you to discontinue your policy.

Selwyn Earning yourself a large bonus.

Peter Why not? I've just moved to an expensive neighbourhood.

Selwyn But Imogen's death changes things, doesn't it? Think carefully. The police will have to be brought in now. If you tell them it wasn't suicide—that John and I murdered her . . .

John I had nothing to do with it!

Selwyn Oh, do stop bobbing up and down, John. (*To Peter*) You knew the original plot to poison my wife's drink.

Peter Yes.

Selwyn Then won't you blush to admit you did nothing to stop it?

Peter I never blush.

Selwyn Not even at being charged as an accessory before the fact?

Peter No.

Selwyn Yet technically you were.

Peter On the contrary. That little green bottle containing the poison . . .

Selwyn Well?

Peter Two days ago, Christine exchanged the contents for some harmless tablets.

Imogen enters from the bedroom

Imogen For which I shall always be eternally grateful.

John Imogen!

Selwyn If you say you passed out I shall sue you for plagiarism.

Imogen No, darling. Like you, I was playing a part. When you predicted I was about to drop dead and I still felt very much alive I knew something had gone wrong.

Selwyn So?

Imogen What would you have done if you'd known that the poison hadn't worked?

Selwyn Thrown you off the balcony, probably.

Imogen Exactly. So I decided on a strategic retreat. I thought my collapse was streets ahead of yours. I shall play Cleopatra next year.

Peter So when I went into the bedroom just now I put her in the picture.

Imogen Dear boy.

Peter And now I have enough proof to get each of you long spells for attempted murder.

John You're not going to turn us in?

Peter I'm hoping that won't be necessary.

Imogen Darling.

Peter I said I'm hoping it isn't.

Selwyn Ah! Here come the conditions.

Peter Naturally, I must put my Company first.

Selwyn And foremost.

Peter And I'm afraid we can't afford to insure such high-risk clients as the Pipers.

Imogen They should have thought of that when they signed us up.

Peter I'm thinking of it now. I'm signing you off.

Selwyn You want us to surrender the policy?

Peter Not surrender. Forfeit. (*He produces a document*) This document renounces all claims on the Company and cancels your policy and your entitlement to surrender value.

Selwyn What? (*He is genuinely outraged*) That is the most unprincipled suggestion I have ever heard!

Peter Then you have a short memory.

Selwyn How dare you suggest that any of my actions this evening were unprincipled! My whole plan was an elementary form of life insurance. It was based on the highest principles of self protection and retribution. For justification I cite the Koran, *Pilgrim's Progress* and at least fourteen chapters of the Old Testament.

Peter Well, I'll read them when I can spare the time. In the meantime, perhaps you'd like to read this.

Selwyn (*taking the document*) Give it to me.

Peter And then sign it.

Imogen What's the alternative?

John He's already touched on that. He goes to the police.

Selwyn Yes—Yet I wonder . . . ?

Peter What?

Selwyn Just how much credence they would place on your story?

Peter That's your risk, isn't it? (*He gives Selwyn a pen*)

Selwyn Thank you. To sign or not to sign? What do you think, John?

John I never did like insurance men and now I know why. Sign the damned thing and be done with it.

Selwyn Imogen?

Imogen It's up to you, Selwyn. I'm no longer your business manager.

Selwyn You still have a half interest.

Imogen I don't mind, as long as you're suffering with me.

Selwyn Very well. Where do I sign?

Peter Where it says signature.

Selwyn I feel terribly let down.

Peter You're giving up a lot of money.

Selwyn Oh damn the money! No, Peter, it's you I'm disappointed in. Apart from myself, you were the only man I ever knew who was never wrong. And now I find you knew all the answers beforehand. You'd filched the exam papers.

Peter Yes, I'm sorry about that.

Selwyn I should hope so. Expulsion's too good for you, my lad. We shall have to think up something even worse. Why do you think I didn't keep the exam paper locked up?

Peter Sign please, Mr Piper.

Selwyn appears to be about to sign, but suddenly begins to laugh

John What the devil are you laughing at?

Selwyn It worked.

John What worked?

Selwyn Shall we tell them, John? Imogen?

John Pardon?

Selwyn Oh come on. We can stop pretending now. They actually fell for it. I told you they would.

Peter Stop wriggling and sign.

Selwyn Sign? Don't talk nonsense. You recall saying that synopsis might be the plot for a novel?

Peter Yes.

Selwyn Well, it was. This entire evening has been a hoax from start to finish—with you and Christine as the victims.

Peter And who were the organizers?

Selwyn The three of us.

Peter To gain what?

Selwyn A plot for the best story I shall ever write.

Peter Come off it!

Selwyn Based on your reactions to what happened.

Peter You're not serious?

Selwyn I'm always serious about my books.

Peter I think you're mad.

Selwyn But not certifiable.

Imogen begins to laugh

Peter Mrs Piper, do you realize what your husband is saying?

Imogen It's obvious, isn't it?

Peter But highly unlikely as you can certainly confirm.

Imogen Yes—but I won't—because it's true. (*She runs to Selwyn*) I think I gave my finest performance, didn't I, darling?

Selwyn Scintillating. In fact the whole evening has been a most successful experiment, don't you agree, John?

John Eh?

Selwyn There you are—the complete affinity between author and publisher. You see? We're unanimous.

Peter Of course. It conveniently clears them both.

Selwyn Just as it clears me. And if we stick to our stories there's nothing you can do about it.

Peter I don't know.

Selwyn Except join in the joke.

Selwyn and Imogen laugh

Peter I wish you'd all stop laughing.

John I'm not laughing.

Imogen Then start.

John begins to laugh reluctantly

Selwyn All life I've been striving for the perfect meld of fact and fiction. They say I write ingenious stories which entertain the reader without ever convincing him they could really happen. Well, now I shall create a masterpiece about this evening with the knowledge that everything in it could, should and did happen.

Peter You haven't convinced me.

Selwyn But I bet you I could convince a jury. Don't you think I'd make a most able defendant?

Imogen Me, too. I'd be ravishing and noble and very, very credible.

Peter But what about John?

Imogen Oh, we wouldn't dream of putting him in the witness box, would we, Selwyn?

Selwyn No. We'd speak for him.

Imogen We always do.

John Thank you very much.

Selwyn So be sensible, Peter. You're outmatched. Call it a day, and I may increase my fire insurance.

Peter Just a minute. You say all this was a game to test our reactions?

Selwyn By George! I think he's got it.

Peter But how could you be sure we'd spot the clues you say you planted? The synopsis, for example?

Selwyn Because, dear reader, a simple device with a piece of cotton told me that Christine had disturbed it.

John Exactly!

Selwyn silences him with a long look

Peter But how could you be sure she'd read it?

Selwyn She's a woman.

Peter All right. Then what?

Selwyn I sent her to you with that fictitious request for insurance information. And, of course, I knew you'd connect the request with the story outline. Have you caught up with me now?

Peter I'm ahead of you. Are you still with us, John?

John Oh yes, all the way.

Peter Ah! There's still the poison.

John Which poison?

Peter The pills in the little green bottle which Christine exchanged for harmless tablets.

Selwyn What about them?

Peter What would you say if I told you I'd had them analysed?

Selwyn And have you?

Peter No.

Selwyn You were convinced they were poison?

Peter Quite. Yet you claim you never intended to poison anyone?

Selwyn I do.

Peter So there'd be no reason to put poison in that bottle?

Selwyn None.

Peter Or in that glass at Imogen's cottage?

Selwyn No.

Imogen He does persist, doesn't he?

Peter (to John) Then why were you so anxious to get rid of it if it was just whisky?

John Quite simple!

Peter Yes?

An excruciating pause

John Tell him, Selwyn.

Selwyn Well—at that stage—our symphony was still unfinished. We were still fascinated by your behaviour. I was sure you hadn't really gone to that restaurant so I sent John to see if you'd follow. Right, John?

John Indeed it is. Why, at one stage I even slowed down to make sure you didn't lose me.

Imogen Don't overplay it, dear.

Selwyn Does that satisfy you, or is there anything else you'd like to know?

Peter I don't think so. But there is one little thing I'd like you to do for me.

Selwyn Only too pleased to help.

Peter We'll see. As you've been conducting an experiment all evening I don't suppose you'd object to my conducting one now.

Selwyn My dear fellow, it would be most ungracious of me to object.

Peter Those little pills which Christine replaced . . .

Selwyn Yes?

Peter (producing a bottle) These are the originals. I kept them just in case. Of course, as you say, they're completely harmless.

John What are you up to, Fletcher?

Selwyn Steady, John. Let our guest have his moment.

Peter I believe you recommend them with whisky.
Selwyn Please yourself.
Peter I'd rather please you. I'm asking *you* to take them.
Selwyn I've been on champagne all evening, but for the experiment I'm
    willing to mix my drinks. (*He goes and pours a drink*)
Imogen Oh goodie, darling—your turn to die!
Selwyn (*to Peter*) And a little water.
Peter Say when.
Imogen Don't drown it.
Peter Water for you too, Douglas?
John You're not asking me to take that stuff?
Peter Why not? It was all a hoax, remember?
Selwyn Yes, John. He wants proof. Let's give it to him.

Peter gives Selwyn a glass

    Aren't you going to join us?
Peter Later, perhaps.
John I will not be involved in something so childish and undignified.
    Besides, how do I know that the original pills were harmless?
Selwyn You have my word.
John I know, but . . .
Selwyn They were quite innocuous.
John Then you drink on your own.
Imogen Oh, John, don't be a spoil-sport.
Selwyn I agree. We've always trusted each other completely—except with
    wives of course.
John I'm just not thirsty.
Selwyn Well, if that's the way you feel . . .
John Fletcher doesn't need two of us to prove his point.
Selwyn Then I wish you, health, wealth . . . (*He raises the glass to his lips*)
Christine No! Don't drink it, please.
Selwyn Christine, why not? You don't think I'd deliberately drink poison,
    do you?
Imogen Of course not. Do drink up, darling. The suspense is unbearable.
Christine Peter, does he have to?
Peter You heard what he said.
Christine Haven't we had enough shocks for one evening?
Peter One more won't kill us.
Selwyn Of course not. (*He hesitates*) However, in deference to Christine's
    wishes, let's do it some other way. (*He picks up the bottle and gives it to
    Peter*) Take this stuff and have it analysed. That will settle the matter
    once and for all. If you read my novels you'll know I always prefer
    science to melodrama.
Peter You're bluffing.
Selwyn How can I be? You have the evidence. Use it.

A long pause

Peter You really mean it, don't you? Yet I can't help thinking . . .

Selwyn I've never been more serious in my life. Take them to a friendly chemist. He'll confirm my story. Go on—I want you to.

Pause

Peter No thanks. You win. (*He puts the bottle of pills on the drinks cabinet and picks up the document*) Come on, darling. We never did have that meal. (*He and Christine go to the door*) And even if it is poison, he'd simply say that was part of the plot too.

Selwyn What a clever idea! You're absolutely wasted in insurance. Don't forget your pen.

Peter Thanks. When you do write that novel, remember to change our names.

Selwyn What shall I call you?

Peter I'm sure you'll think of something.

Peter and Christine leave through the main door

Imogen They believed you. They actually believed you!

John You were superb, Selwyn. You know for a moment you almost had me fooled.

Selwyn Really?

Imogen But don't let it go to your head, Selwyn. I shan't forget that you tried to kill me and I shall return the compliment, believe me.

Selwyn You wouldn't.

Imogen Oh yes, I would.

Selwyn Imogen, your vindictiveness grieves me. Particularly in view of my complete innocence.

Imogen Innocence!

Selwyn Yes. Everything I told Fletcher was true.

John Eh?

Selwyn As far as it went. I merely omitted to say that besides manipulating him I had you and John on a string as well.

Imogen Oh, come on. You've had your fun. You've convinced them. You don't have to convince us as well.

Selwyn It's true.

John He means it. I really believe he means it!

Selwyn Of course I do.

John Then why didn't you tell me?

Selwyn I wanted to study you—observe your behaviour. And what a fascinating specimen you turned out to be.

John Listen to him! I warned you about Imogen. If it wasn't for me you'd be dead.

Selwyn I grant you that, but what interesting shades of character you revealed in the process. What do they call a man who'd murder his mistress for fifty thousand pounds?

Imogen Rich?

Selwyn Or a wife who tries to kill her husband for the same amount?

Imogen Dear, stainless Selwyn. The one little innocent among us.

Selwyn Right.

Imogen Well, I know damn well you tried to poison me. I saw the look on your face when you thought I was dying.

Selwyn I'm sure it was most affectionate.

Imogen If I hadn't pretended to faint, what would you have done?

Selwyn Watched you pass the worst few minutes of your life. A mild punishment for trying to put an end to mine.

Imogen God, I hate you . . . (*To John*) And I loathe you!

Selwyn Stop it—you know I detest favouritism. Anyway, I've got what I wanted—my next book. So as I'm feeling very benign, let's see if I can't give you both what you want. Starting with Imogen. How about an uncontested divorce?

Imogen Are you serious?

Selwyn If you still want it.

Imogen I'll drink to that. (*She goes to the drinks cabinet, pours out three drinks and—unseen by the audience, puts pills in two of them*) You're very prudent, Selwyn.

Selwyn I think we could all do with a drink. And now you, John. I suppose I do owe you something. Apart from my next best seller.

John I just want to forget about this whole damned business.

Selwyn And so you shall, my dear chap, as long as you don't read my book. But I know you will. Your curiosity will get the better of you. Anyway, it'll make you a fortune.

Imogen (*handing a glass to Selwyn*) Champagne, husband. (*Then a glass to John*) Brandy, lover.

Selwyn Don't you agree, darling?

Imogen About what?

Selwyn John's curiosity. He'll read the book all right.

John No, I shan't. Not a single, solitary word.

Selwyn Not even the price?

Imogen You know somehow I don't think I'll read it either.

Selwyn Nonsense—I'll send you a copy. Vitriolically inscribed, of course.

Imogen There'll be no point. I know the plot.

Selwyn Are you sure? Was it all a hoax, or did I really try to poison you?

Imogen I don't need the book to know that.

Selwyn You sound very sure of yourself.

Selwyn and John drink

Imogen I am. Or I shall be in a few seconds.

Selwyn and John look at her as she holds up the bottle of pills

Yes, darlings. The original tablets.

They look at their drinks, and then at each other

You should be going any minute now.

Imogen imitates Selwyn looking at his watch at the end of ACT II, SCENE 1, *as—*

the CURTAIN *falls*

FURNITURE AND PROPERTY LIST

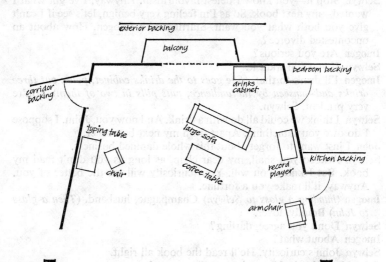

exterior backing

balcony

corridor backing

bedroom backing

drinks cabinet

typing table

large sofa

chair

coffee table

record player

kitchen backing

armchair

ACT I

On stage: Large sofa. *On it:* cushions
    Armchair
    Coffee-table. *On it:* copy of *Life* magazine, face down
    Typing table. *On it:* typewriter, paper, pile of letters for posting, tele-
       phone, one or two books, dressing. *Below it:* waste-paper basket
    Upright chair
    Record player with records
    Drinks cabinet. *On it:* assorted drinks including whisky, brandy, gin,
       soda syphon, water, assorted glasses, dish of nuts. *Hidden from
       sight:* bucket containing opened bottle of champagne with patent
       removable stopper
    Other furnishings as desired
    In bedroom door: key (offstage)
    In kitchen door: key
    On main door: frame with card on outside
    Carpet
    Window curtains

Personal: **Selwyn:** wristwatch, patent rubber ball strapped to armpit, bottle of
tablets, handkerchiefs
Imogen: dark glasses, handbag with revolver, paper-knife, silk scarf
Christine: key

ACT II
Scene 1

Off stage: Whisky bottle wrapped in tissue **(Selwyn)**

Scene 2

Off stage: Typed pages **(Peter)**
Document **(Peter)**
Small bottle **(Peter)**

Personal: **Peter:** pen

LIGHTING PLOT

Property fittings required: wall brackets (dressing only)

Interior. A drawing-room. The same scene throughout

ACT I   Early evening

To open: General effect of bright early autumn evening
No cues

ACT II, SCENE 1. Early evening

To open: As previous act
No cues

ACT II, SCENE 2. Early morning

To open: As previous scene
No cues

EFFECTS PLOT

ACT I

Cue 1   **Selwyn** pours drink   (Page 5)
Doorbell rings

Cue 2   **Imogen** tries the bedroom door   (Page 9)
Doorbell rings

Cue 3   **Peter:** "Will you forgive me?"   (Page 14)
Doorbell rings

Cue 4   **Christine:** "Not with an appointment."   (Page 14)
Doorbell rings

Cue 5   **Peter:** "Yes, Mr Douglas, what do you mean?"   (Page 17)
Doorbell rings

ACT II

Scene 1

Cue 6   **Selwyn** puts on record   (Page 31)
Music: "Bye-bye Blues"

Cue 7   **Selwyn** and **Imogen** kiss   (Page 33)
Telephone rings

Cue 8   **Selwyn** stops record-player   (Page 33)
Music off

Cue 9   **Selwyn** puts on record   (Page 34)
Music: "They Can't Take That Away From Me" (*non-vocal*)

Scene 2

Cue 10   As Curtain rises   (Page 36)
Continue previous music from record-player

Cue 11   **Selwyn** picks up magazine   (Page 36)
Doorbell rings

Cue 12   **Selwyn** stops record-player   (Page 36)
Music off

Cue 13   **Selwyn:** ". . . a healthy preponderance of snakes."   (Page 37)
Doorbell rings

Cue 14   **Selwyn:** "All catered for."   (Page 37)
Doorbell rings

MADE AND PRINTED IN GREAT BRITAIN BY
LATIMER TREND & COMPANY LTD PLYMOUTH
MADE IN ENGLAND